THE HUTCHINSON
DICTIONARY
of
ENGLISH USAGE

THE HUTCHINSON
DICTIONARY
of
ENGLISH USAGE

ВВ Bounty
Books

First published in 1995 by Helicon Publishing

This edition published in 2006 by Bounty Books,
a division of Octopus Publishing Group Ltd,
2-4 Heron Quays, London E14 4JP,
by arrangement with Helicon Publishing

ISBN-13: 978 0 753711 19 4
ISBN-10: 0 753711 19 2

A CIP catalogue record for this book is available from
the British Library

Printed and bound in Great Britain

ACKNOWLEDGEMENTS

Managing Editor	Hilary McGlynn
Consultant Editor	Andrew Delahunty
Project Editor	D'Arcy Adrian-Vallance
Contributors	John Ayto
	Jessica Feinstein
	Fred McDonald
	Carole Owen
	Adrian Room
Screen Editor	Avril Cridlan
Production	Tony Ballsdon
Design and Page makeup	Roger Walker

INTRODUCTION

This guide sets out to give clear, straightforward advice on avoiding errors in spoken and written English.

Most people are at some time uncertain or confused about which word to use in a particular context, how to pronounce or spell a word, or whether they are using a word in the correct meaning. The guide aims to help you choose the right word or the most appropriate way of expressing yourself.

The entries cover the following areas of usage:

meanings Is it correct to use the word *aggravate* to mean 'make worse' or to use *locate* to mean 'find'?

confusables What is the difference between *complement* and *compliment*? Or between *flaunt* and *flout*?

grammar Is it *different from*; *different to* or *different than*? Why do some people regard it as wrong to split infinitives?

punctuation What are the rules about using the comma, the apostrophe, quotation marks, etc?

parts of speech What exactly is a preposition? Or a participle?

style What is the right way to set out a business letter? How can you ensure that your writing is non-sexist?

spellings Should it be *-ise* or *-ize*? Which is correct, *miniscule* or *minuscule*?

pronunciation What is the right way to pronounce such words as *controversy; lichen; macho*?

All entries in the guide are arranged alphabetically, whether dealing with individual words such as *anticipate* or *hopefully*, or topics such as *American English* or *letter writing*.

While recommendations are given wherever possible, the entries generally avoid making a simplistic and didactic distinction between correct and incorrect usage. Language is changing all the time, and some usages that were once disapproved of are now widely accepted as perfectly good English. Equally, some uses that are natural and common in informal contexts may be considered inappropriate in formal contexts.

The entries attempt to explain where there is some dispute surrounding a particular word or construction and to state clearly which usages are acceptable in formal English, which are acceptable in informal English, and which are still generally considered to be wrong. Where there are significant differences between British and American usage these are clearly explained.

a _or_ an A is used before consonants, **an** before a vowel sound. _A_ comes before words that begin with a **u**, but are pronounced as though they began with a **y**: _a union; a useful gadget._ _An_ comes before a silent **h**: _an heir; an honour._ Some people still use _an_ before **h** in words from French, where the **h** was silent: _an hotel._ This is rather old-fashioned. There is no reason to use _an_ before an **h** which is sounded.

abbreviations Abbreviations are used to save time and space, and to make long names of organizations and long technical terms easier to remember and less tedious to refer to repeatedly in an extended piece of writing such as a newspaper article or textbook. In such contexts, if the abbreviation is not a very common one, the long name or technical term is often given in full at the first mention, with the abbreviation in brackets after it. After that just the abbreviation is used.

Every day more and more abbreviations appear, and old ones die. No sooner had we learned to refer to the Common Market as the EC rather than the EEC, than it became the EU.

Generally it is acceptable to write abbreviations either with or without full stops, but the trend is towards leaving them out, as in _BBC, Dr, HoD, H E Bates, Prof E Potter._ Punchy writing such as that found in advertisements tends to leave out full stops, whereas formal non-technical writing is more traditional, and full stops are often used.

There are various kinds of abbreviation. The most common is the set of initials, for example _DIY_ for Do It Yourself, _DSS_ for Department of Social Security, _gbh_ for grievous bodily harm, _JCB_ for a machine invented by Joseph Cyril Bamford.

Some abbreviations are the first part of a longer word and are pronounced as words, not said as a sequence of letters of the alphabet. Examples are _ad_ and _advert_ from advertisement, _bra_ from brassière, _gym_ from gymnasium, and _limo_ from limousine.

Other abbreviations made by cutting off the end of the word are not used in speech, for example _adv_ for adverb and _cont_ for continued. If these need to be read aloud, they are read as the unabbreviated full forms.

Some words lose bits in the middle. *Bdg* stands for building; *Chas* for Charles. *Dr, ft, Mr,* and *Mrs* are other examples. These are read aloud as their unabbreviated full forms.

A few words lop off the first part, for example *bus* and *plane*, though these are now so well established that they are really no longer thought of as reduced forms, but as words in their own right.

There is a significant proportion of abbreviations which it is possible for an English speaker to pronounce as words rather than as sequences of letters of the alphabet. For example, *NATO* is said [**nay**-toe] and never [en eh tee oh]. Sets of initials like *NATO*, and new forms made up of the first parts of two or more words, such as *OXFAM*, are called **acronyms**. Further examples are *UNESCO, Amstrad, GATT, ACORN, dinky, Aids, laser, ERNIE,* and *CLEAR.* A few abbreviations are pronounced both ways, *VAT* being the prime example.

Acronyms are often new words. The word *Nato* did not exist before it began to be used as a quick way of referring to the North Atlantic Treaty Organization. It is not, in fact, a very typical English word, although it is easy enough for English speakers to pronounce. *COHSE,* the Confederation of Health Service Employees, looks un-English, but is pronounced [cosy].

Laser, on the other hand, looks thoroughly at home in English. There are probably many people who are quite unaware that it is an acronym, derived from: light amplification by stimulated emission of radiation. The fact that it is not written in capital letters, and is a common noun rather than the name of an organization, also helps to disguise it. This is the sort of acronym that easily makes its way into a dictionary. *Yuppie,* from: young upwardly mobile professional; and *radar,* from: Radio Detection and Ranging, are other examples.

Some acronyms are existing words taken over as more easily used alternatives to full forms, *ACORN,* for example, which stands for: A Classification of Residential Neighbourhoods, a sampling system based on different kinds of dwelling; or *AIDS,* from: acquired immune deficiency syndrome; or *WASP,* from: White Anglo-Saxon Protestant.

Some organizations deliberately choose terms for products, projects, or equipment so that the initials will make an existing name. An example of this is *ERNIE,* from: Electronic Random Number Indicator Equipment. This is the machine that chooses the winners of Premium Bonds. A *TESSA* is a Tax Exempt Savings Bond. These short and friendly-sounding names suggest something pleasant and accessible.

Another case of image manipulation by acronym is the choice of the title Fast Reactor Experiment, Dounreay to give *FRED*.

Campaigning organizations, in particular, choose names to yield an acronym that is suggestive of their aims. *ASH*, Action on Smoking and Health wants people to stop smoking; *GASP* is the Group Against Smog Pollution; *SCUM*, the Society for Cutting Up Men, wants to attract your attention.

The form in which acronyms are written varies. The small number that are common nouns rather than names are often found in small letters, and become indistinguishable from words. These are nouns such as *laser*, *radar*, and *aids*. The plural is made, as with most ordinary words, by simply adding **s**, for example *KOs, JCBs, lasers*. No apostrophe is needed.

Names of organizations are most often written as a string of capital letters without full stops, but practice is variable, and you may see *Unesco* or unesco as well as *UNESCO*. You may even see *U.N.E.S.C.O.*.

Note that not all abbreviations that could be acronyms are so in fact. *BA*, for example, is always said [bee eh] and never [bar]. A particularly interesting case is *ETA*. When it means 'Estimated Time of Arrival' it is an abbreviation, and is pronounced [ee tee eh], but when it stands for the Basque separatist group it is an acronym, and is pronounced [etter], to rhyme with *better*.

One problem with abbreviations that are pronounceable as words is that when you meet a new one in print, you may not know which way to say it. This is more of a problem now that all abbreviations, not just acronyms, tend to be written without full stops. A full stop after each letter usually means that the abbreviation is pronounced as a string of letters.

abdicate, abrogate, arrogate *or* **derogate** To **abdicate** is to renounce formally, especially a monarch the throne: *Edward VIII abdicated in order to marry a divorcee*; *She abdicated her rights to a pension*. To **abrogate** a law is to cancel or annul it: *The old law on Sunday trading has been abrogated*. To **arrogate** a thing is to claim it presumptuously or without right: *He arrogated special privileges for the staff*. To **derogate** a thing is to lessen or detract from it in some way: *It would derogate from the park's attraction to compare it to a playground*.

aberration Spelling: remember one **b** and two **r**s.

abhor Spelling: remember the **h**.

abhorrent Spelling: remember the **h** and the ending **-ent**.

abjure *or* **adjure** To **abjure** something is to renounce it or abstain from it, with the implication that this is done publicly: *Members of the sect were required to abjure all alcoholic drink.* To **adjure** someone to do something is to request them solemnly to do it: *The magistrate adjured the witness to tell the truth frankly.*

-able *or* **-ible** See ⟩spelling rules.

abominable Spelling: note the single **b** and **m**.

abridgement *or* **abridgment** This word can be spelled either way.

abrogate See ⟩abdicate.

abscess Spelling: remember the **sc** in the middle.

abstinent *or* **abstemious** Abstinent relates to abstaining or holding back from something, especially food and (alcoholic) drink: *He holds that it is good for the body to be abstinent from time to time.* **Abstemious** means not taking too much food and (alcoholic) drink: *His abstemious habits do not prevent him from enjoying parties.*

abuse *or* **misuse** To **abuse** something is to use it badly or wrongly: *The bank manager abused the confidence of his customers.* To **misuse** a thing is to use it in a way for which it was not intended, whether wrongly or not: *'A horse misused upon the road/Calls to Heaven for human blood'* (William Blake).

abysmal Spelling: remember **y**, not **i**.

abyss Spelling: remember **y**, not **i**.

accede *or* **concede** To **accede** to something is to agree to it: *I accede to your request* (I accept it); to **concede** something is to accept it grudgingly or reluctantly: *I concede your superiority* (I have to admit you are better). Spelling: remember the ending **-cede**.

accelerate Spelling: note the two **c**s and one **l**.

accept *or* **except** To **accept** something or someone is to take them: *Credit cards are accepted* (you can use them to pay); to **except** them is to exclude them: *Credit cards are excepted* (you'll have to pay by cash or cheque).

accessory *or* **accessary** Accessory is the normal spelling of the word to mean something extra or additional: *The vacuum cleaner had several accessory parts.* In the legal sense, however, the spelling

accessary is sometimes found: *She was charged with being an accessary to the crime* (she had taken a part in it). In the USA, **accessory** is the spelling for both senses.

accommodation Spelling: note the double **c** and double **m**.

accord *or* **accordance** If a thing is in **accord** with something else, it is in agreement with it: *The contract is in full accord with company policy* (it agrees with it). If a thing is in **accordance** with something else, it obeys or follows it: *The contract was drawn up in accordance with your instructions* (as you directed).

accrue This is sometimes used to mean simply 'grow' or 'increase'. It actually means 'to grow or increase by regular increments'; interest **accrues** in a bank account as amounts are added to it at set intervals.

accumulate Spelling: note the two **c**s and one **m**.

accusative case The case of a noun or pronoun that is the object of a verb or is governed by a preposition. *Me, him, her, us,* and *them* are the accusative forms of the pronouns *I, he, she, we,* and *they.*

acknowledgement *or* **acknowledgment** This word can be spelled either way.

acoustic Spelling: note the single **c**.

acquainted Spelling: remember the **c**.

acquiesce Spelling: remember the **c** at the beginning and the **sc** at the end.

acquire Spelling: remember the **c**.

acronym A word formed from the initial letters and/or syllables of other words, intended as a pronounceable abbreviation; for example *NATO* (North Atlantic Treaty Organization) and *radar* (radio detecting and ranging). See ◊abbreviations.

acrylic Spelling: note the **y**.

active The form of a verb where the subject of the sentence performs the action: *Alan caught the dog* (rather than *The dog was caught by Alan*). See also ◊passive.

actually This can be used for emphasis or to express indignation: *He actually called me a liar*. It is also used instead of *really*: *He may seem a bit simple, but actually he's quite shrewd*. Avoid using it unnecessarily where no emphasis is called for: *Actually, I've never met the Queen*.

acumen *or* **acuity** Acumen is the ability to understand or appreciate things quickly and clearly: *To become an MP it helps to have political acumen*. **Acuity** is sharpness or keenness of thought or of the senses: *The hawk has great acuity of sight*.

address Spelling: remember the double **d** and double **s**.

adjacent *or* **adjoining** If one thing is **adjacent** to another, it is next to it without necessarily making physical contact: *The car park was adjacent to the sports hall*. An **adjoining** object, however, has a common point of contact with another: *The offices are to the left, with a canteen adjoining*.

adjective This is a grammatical part of speech for words that describe nouns (for example, new and beautiful, as in *a new hat* and *a beautiful day*). Adjectives generally have three degrees (grades or levels for the description of relationships): the positive degree: *new, beautiful*, the comparative degree: *newer, more beautiful*, and the superlative degree: *newest, most beautiful*.

Some adjectives do not normally need comparative and superlative forms; one person cannot be *more asleep* than someone else, a lone action is unlikely to be *the most single-handed action ever seen*, and many people dislike the expression *most unique* or *almost unique*, because something unique is supposed to be the only one that exists. For purposes of emphasis or style these conventions may be set aside: *I don't know who is more unique; they are both remarkable people*.

Double comparatives such as *more bigger* are not grammatical in Standard English, but Shakespeare used a double superlative: *'the most unkindest cut of all' (Julius Caesar)*. Some adjectives may have both comparative and both superlative forms *commoner and more common; commonest and most common*; shorter words usually take on the suffixes **-er/-est** but occasionally they may be given the *more/most* forms for emphasis or other reasons: *Which of them is the most clear?*.

When an adjective comes before a noun it is attributive; when it comes after noun and verb (for example, *It looks good*) it is predicative. Some adjectives can only be used predicatively: *The child was asleep*, but not: *the asleep child*. The participles of verbs are regularly used adjectivally: *a sleeping child; boiled milk*, often in compound forms: *a quick-acting medicine; a glass-making factory; a hard-boiled egg; well-trained teachers*. Adjectives are often formed by adding suffixes to nouns: *sand: sandy; nation: national*.

adjoining See ◊adjacent.

adjourn Spelling: note the **d**, and the **ou** as in *journey*.

admirable The standard pronunciation is with the stress on the first syllable [**add**-mruh-ble].

admit It used to be considered incorrect to use *to* after *admit* in the sense 'confess', but it is now widely accepted when referring to an action: *he admitted the crime* or *he admitted to the crime. To* should be avoided when referring to a quality or when *admit* is followed by a verb: *she admitted her guilt*; *I admit lying about this matter*.

ad nauseam Spelling: note the ending **-eam**, not **-eum**.

adolescent Spelling: note the **c**.

adverb This is a grammatical part of speech for words that modify or describe verbs: *she ran quickly*, adjectives: *a beautifully clear day*, and adverbs: *they did it really well*. Most adverbs are formed from adjectives or past participles by adding **-ly**: *quick: quickly* or **-ally**: *automatic: automatically*.

Sometimes adverbs are formed by adding **-wise** as in *moving clockwise*; (in the phrase *a clockwise direction, clockwise* is an adjective). Some adverbs have a distinct form from their partnering adjective, for example, *good/well*: *it was good work; they did it well*. Others do not derive from adjectives, for example *very*, in *very nice*; *tomorrow*, in *I'll do it tomorrow*. Some are unadapted adjectives, for example *pretty*, as in *It's pretty good*). Sentence adverbs modify whole sentences or phrases: *Generally, it rains a lot here*; *Usually, the town is busy at this time of year*.

Adverbs are divided into four types, depending on whether they express manner, degree, time, or place. Overuse of adverbs should be avoided. For example, in the sentence *He swiped wildly and the ball whizzed quickly*, the adverbs are redundant, since the verbs contain their meanings already. See also ◊tautology.

adversary The standard British pronunciation is with the stress on the first syllable [**add**-vuh-sree]. The US pronunciation also has the stress on the first syllable, but both **r**s are pronounced, and the end is pronounced [serry] to rhyme with *sherry*.

advisable Spelling: remember the ending **-able**.

aerial Spelling: remember the **ae** as in aeroplane.

aesthetic *or* **ascetic** **Aesthetic** relates to what is beautiful or artistic: *The architect designed the shopping mall with both aesthetic and practical considerations in mind.* **Ascetic** relates to abstinence from worldly pleasures or creature comforts, often with the aim of spiritual gain: *As a non-smoker and teetotaller he leads a very ascetic life.*

affect *or* **effect** To **affect** something is to have an effect on it: *Smoking can affect your health.* To **effect** something is to make it happen: *The doctor's treatment effected an immediate improvement in the patient's health. Affect* is often used instead of *effect*, so take care when you are writing.

aficionado Spelling: remember there are no double letters.

ageing *or* **aging** This word can be spelled either way, although **ageing** is more common.

aggravate The main meaning of this word is 'make worse': *Such remarks only serve to aggravate the situation.* It is also commonly used to mean 'annoy' or 'exasperate': *It really aggravates me the way you always interrupt.* Although this second use dates back to the 16th century, some people still disapprove of it.

aggressive Spelling: note the double g.

aging See ◊ageing.

agnostic *or* **atheist** An **agnostic** is someone who holds that it is impossible to know whether there is a God or not. An **atheist** holds that there is no God. The word agnostic was invented by the 19th-century biologist T H Huxley.

agoraphobia Spelling: remember the **ora**.

agreement In grammar, the harmony whereby parts of a sentence agree in number, gender, and case. The form of a verb depends on the nature of its grammatical subject. This can vary in two basic ways: number – it can be singular or plural; and person – it can be first person, second person or third person. To find out more about these, look at the entries for ◊number and ◊person.

aisle The s is silent, and the word rhymes with *smile.* Spelling: remember the s.

alias *or* **alibi** An **alias** is a false name, not a false description or personation: *His real name was John Smith but he ran his business under the alias of Joe Bloggs.* An **alibi** is properly a statement that a person was somewhere else at the time a crime was committed: *His alibi was supported by his sister, who had been visiting him that evening.* It can also be used of a general excuse: *My alibi is that the train was late.* However, this is thought unacceptable by some people.

align Spelling: note the single **l** and the **g**.

allay, alleviate, *or* **assuage** To **allay** something is to make it less or get rid of it altogether: *She allayed my fears by saying that she also had heard nothing; I want to allay any doubts you may have about this.* To **alleviate** is to relieve something unpleasant or painful by making it less severe: *The ointment soon alleviated the discomfort; Volunteer workers did their best to alleviate the situation.* To **assuage** is similar, but is mainly used of unpleasant emotions or bodily sensations: *I tried to assuage the old man's terror; The crew were desperate to assuage their fearful thirst.*

allege Spelling: note that there is no **d**.

alleviate See ▷allay.

alliteration Spelling: note the double **l** and single **t**.

all right *or* **alright** *The answers are all right* may mean that all of them are correct or that they are satisfactory on the whole. Some people would like to use **alright** to avoid confusion, but **all right** is considered correct. It is possible that *alright* will one day be accepted (as *already* and *altogether* have been), but for now it is better to rewrite the sentence: *all the answers are right* or *the answers are satisfactory*.

alternately *or* **alternatively** Alternately means 'one after another, by turns': *We worked and rested alternately.* **Alternatively** means 'instead of that': *We could walk. Alternatively, we could go by bus.*

alternative Some people feel that, because it is derived from the Latin *alter*, meaning 'one or the other of two', *alternative* should be used only when the choice is between two things or courses of action. But **alternative** and **alternatively** can be used with more than two: *There are several alternatives; Come to lunch. Alternatively, I could come to your house, or we could meet somewhere.*

alternatively See ▷alternately.

aluminium US spelling: *aluminum*.

ambiguous *or* **ambivalent** If something is **ambiguous** it has more than one possible meaning, and so is obscure or difficult to understand:

When I asked Stuart if he condemned my action he gave me an ambiguous answer; The message was perfectly clear and not in the least ambiguous. If a person is **ambivalent** they have an uncertain attitude or feeling towards someone or something: *The French are ambivalent about royalty: they abolished their own monarchy but are very interested in the British royal family*. A common error is to use *ambivalent* instead of *ambiguous*.

amen The standard pronunciation in Britain is [ah-**men**], although Roman Catholics tend to favour a pronunciation in which the first syllable rhymes with *day*. In the USA this is the usual pronunciation, but [ah-**men**] is used in singing.

amend *or* **emend** To **amend** something is to alter it, usually for the better: *The referee amended certain rules to make it easier for the new players*. To **emend** something is to correct it, especially a printed text: *The editor emended the text, which was full of errors*.

America This is used rather loosely with several different meanings. It can refer to the USA or to the USA and Canada, or to the whole land mass of North, South, and Central America. It is best to be precise: use *United States*, *US*, or *USA* (*the States* is acceptable in informal speech), *North America* for the USA and Canada, *Central America* for the area from Mexico to Panama, *South America* for the continent to the south, and *the Americas* for the whole lot. **American** is the only adjective available to describe someone or something from the USA; be careful to make it clear if you are referring to some other part of the Americas.

American English

In July 1994 a British MP proposed in the House of Commons a bill banning the use in English of words borrowed from French. There was laughter in the House as he spelled out the implications: no more croissants or baguettes, no hors d'œuvres, no visits to cafés or brasseries; in fact, no restaurants. No more rendez-vous, affaires, or ménages à trois.

The point of the MP's proposal, made tongue in cheek, was that the French were being chauvinist and absurd in their attempts to keep English expressions out of French. Words taken from other languages can be useful if they label aspects of our experience not already named, or if they provide an enlivening or entertaining metaphor, or an attention-grabbing phrase. Borrowings can enrich a culture. No language is an island, and where two cultures meet, words cross over.

1. Vocabulary

The British MPs laughed at the proposal to ban French words from English, but would they have responded with such hilarity to a proposal to ban Americanisms from British English? American English, like French, has given us many useful words. Surely British English would be the poorer without *boarding house*, *commuter*, *flashpoint*, *gimmick*, *punchline*, *snoop*, *teenager*, or expressions such as *face the music*, *be out on a limb*, *pull the wool over someone's eyes*, *take a back seat*.

Which of the following words or expressions have come into British English from American English? *influential*; *reliable*; *grapevine*; *to advocate*; *to bark up the wrong tree*; *hangover*; *to knuckle down*; *lengthy*; *live wire*; *immigrant*; *hot air*; *to make up your mind*? Well, all of them, actually.

The assimilated words remain because they are useful; and the process of transfer goes on. There are various reasons for this. The USA is the dominant world power. It exports its way of life – so we gained *burgers* and *chewing gum*, *motels* and *BLTs* (bacon, lettuce and tomato sandwiches), *gameshows* and *chatshows*.

The USA leads the world in many technologies. Thus we gained many computer terms, for example *GIGO*, an acronym that stands for 'Garbage In, Garbage Out', and sums up a basic principle of computer use.

Political events in the USA are news in most countries. From *Watergate* we gained the combining form – *gate*, which can be added to any name around which a public scandal centres. For example, for a brief period British newspapers were full of *Dianagate* when an alleged tapescript of a private conversation of Princess Diana's was published.

The USA has a flourishing literature, which is widely read in other English-speaking countries. It is a big producer of English-language films and television programmes, which it sells abroad. The USA is a dynamic culture, creating new words because it is constantly creating new products and new ideas.

Some words are easily recognized as American: *bimbo*, *cop out*, and *guy*, for example. The word *scam*, meaning a swindle, was felt to be sufficiently foreign to be put inside quotation marks when it was used in an article in the Times in 1994. *Rubbernecking* is an American coinage that means turning your head and staring, especially when you are a driver. Traffic news on British radio sometimes now mentions *rubbernecking accidents*, that is, new accidents caused by drivers turning their heads to look at accidents on the other carriageway.

Most of us know certain American words not used in British contexts, words for everyday things having a different British word. The following pairs will be familiar:

American English	British English
bathrobe	dressing-gown
candies	sweets
checkers	draughts
cookie	biscuit
faucet	tap
gas	petrol
grade	form
mail	post
movie	film
railroad	railway
sidewalk	pavement

There are, however, many more words that are quite run-of- the-mill words for Americans, but which are unknown to most British people. Are you familiar with *the boondocks* (an uninhabited area where the vegetation is thick) or a duplex (an apartment on two floors with stairs to connect them)?

Words which exist in British English, but which have a different meaning in American English, can be very confusing. For a British person a *purse* is a small container for coins, not a handbag, as it is in the USA. In the USA *pants* are trousers, not underpants. A word which is a particularly nasty trap is *billion*, which means a thousand million in the USA. In Britain it used to mean a million million, but British usage is now increasingly following American.

British English has always taken words from one word class and made them work in another. Nouns often become verbs. We *bottle* fruit, *catalogue* goods, and *floor* our opponents. But it is thanks to American facility in this kind of word formation that people *park* their cars, journalists *interview* people, and politicians *advocate* sanctions.

Some words have entered American English from the languages of its non-British settlers. The Spanish *patio* came into American English in the 1820s, *macho* in the 1920s. Italian has given much to American cooking, and the borrowings from Italian reflect this. *Bologna*, for example, is a cooked and smoked sausage made from minced beef and pork. French has given *chowder*, a soup containing fish, milk, and potatoes.

2. Grammar

Grammatical differences between British and American English are minimal. Perhaps the main one is the American use of the past tense where British English would use the present perfect tense. An American might ask, *Did you collect your ticket yet?* where a British person would ask, *Have you collected your ticket yet?*

The present subjunctive is used more in American English than in British English, for example *He proposed that she remain in charge.* A British person would be more likely to use *He proposed that she should remain in charge.*

A few verbs are different: American English has *snuck* where British English has *sneaked*, and *dove* where British English has *dived*. And everybody knows about *gotten*, which for most senses of *get* is an alternative to *got* as the past participle of *get* in American English, although its use is criticized by some Americans.

In British English the general personal pronoun *one* is used, by the upper classes and educated people, as in this example: *One doesn't like to interfere. After all, one wouldn't like to be accused of exceeding one's brief.* American English would start with *one* in the same way, but would follow it with *he* and possessive *his*.

Americans say *Do you have ...?* where many British people say *Have you got ...?* And there are a few differences in the use of prepositions. American English has *different **than*** and *meet **with*** where British English has *different **from*** and simply *meet* (someone).

3. Spelling

There are a few regular differences between British and American spelling. American English keeps a single consonant where British English doubles in all forms derived from words ending in l: *traveled*; *traveling*; *traveler*. However, the following words have double l in American English: *enroll*; *enrollment*; *fulfill*; *installment*.

British English **-our** is American English **-or**: *color*; *humor*. Words that end in **-re** in British English have **-er** in American English: *center*; *theater*. However, **-re** is used to show the hard sound of a preceding c or g: *acre*; *ogre*.

Americans are more inclined than British people to use e rather than ae or oe: *hemoglobin; peony*. They prefer **-ize** to **-ise** at the end of verbs: *organize*. They are less likely to use hyphens in compound nouns: *lookout*.

4. Summary

American English should not be regarded as a corrupt form of British English. Since the major settlement of the USA by English speakers, the two varieties have evolved separately to some extent, though continue to influence each other. The USA has its own standard grammatical forms, spellings, and pronunciations, and these are taught to young Americans with rather more conviction than standard English is taught to young Britons. In some cases, the word *gotten* for example, it is American English which has retained old usages, and British English which has changed.

among *or* **amongst** Some people make a distinction between these, using **amongst** with verbs that imply movement: *we stood among the trees* but: *we walked amongst the trees*; *the money was shared out amongst the members*. There is no need to do so; either form can be used in any context. See also ▷between.

amoral See ▷immoral.

an See ▷a.

analogous The main stress is on the second syllable. The **g** is hard as in *go*, and should not be pronounced like the **j** in [jam].

ancillary Spelling: note the double **l**, and no **i** after the **l**s.

and/or This is useful where it is essential to save space; *dogs and/or cats* is much shorter than *dogs or cats, or both*. It is quite at home on forms, but looks out of place in ordinary writing.

annex *or* **annexe** Spelling: remember that **annex** is a verb, and **annexe** is a noun.

anorexia Spelling: note the **o**.

antarctic The **c** in the middle of this word should be pronounced and should not be forgotten when the word is spelled.

ante- *or* **anti-** Remember that **ante-** means before and **anti-** means against or opposite. This should help you spell such words as:

antecedent
antenatal
anteroom
antibiotic
anticlimax
anticlockwise

anticipate The primary meaning of this is to foresee an event and to take some action to prepare for it or to prevent it: *He had anticipated the question, and had his answer ready*. The meaning 'expect', 'look forward to', although it has been in use since the 18th century, is still considered by some people to be incorrect.

any When the pronoun *any* refers to a single thing, it takes a singular verb: *Is any of that jelly left?* When it is used with reference to a group of people or things, it is usual to use a plural verb: *Are any of your friends coming?* It is perfectly correct and acceptable to use a singular verb, but this tends to sound rather stiff and formal: *Is any of your friends coming?*

When the adjective *any* is applied to a singular noun referring to a person, it may not be clear whether the person is male or female. Traditionally, the pronoun *he* has been used in such contexts: *Any member who wishes to renew his subscription should go to the office*, but in present-day English it is widely felt to be invidious to implicitly exclude women in this way, and it is becoming increasingly common to use *they* instead: *Any member who wishes to renew their subscription should go to the office*. The same applies to the pronouns **anybody** and **anyone**: *I can't believe that anyone would willingly spend their holidays there*.

apartheid The standard British pronunciation is [a-**part**-hate], though pronunciations of the last syllable as [height], [eight], [ite], and [ide] are also heard. Americans pronounce the **r** but do not pronounce the **h**.

aplomb Spelling: remember the silent **b**.

apostasy The stress is on the second syllable [uh-**poss**-tuh-see]. Spelling: note the ending **-asy**, not **-acy**.

apostrophe This is a punctuation mark (') used to indicate either a missing letter *mustn't* for 'must not' or grammatical possession *John's camera*; *people's houses*; *dogs' collars*.

The latter usage (to indicate possession) causes widespread difficulty and the apostrophe crops up in all kinds of incorrect and unlikely places. The apostrophe to indicate possession should be placed on the owner, not the owned; for example, *those boys' bikes*, not *those boys bike's*.

When used to show possession, there is one infallible rule for deciding where the apostrophe goes on the owner. If a final **s** is used for plural, the apostrophe goes outside: *Her coat was left in the ladies' locker room*. When the plural is formed without **s**, *the apostrophe goes on the inside: women's hats*; *men's shoes*; *children's swings*.

Apostrophes are not used to form the plural of words: *Keep These Door's Shut*; *Apple's 56p* – this kind of error is sometimes known as the 'greengrocer's apostrophe'.

appal Spelling: note the double **p** and single **l**, but remember **appalled** and **appalling**.

apparatus Spelling: remember the double **p**.

appearance Spelling: remember the double **p**.

appetite Spelling: remember **e** not **a** after the double **p**.

apposition In grammar, the placing of a noun or noun phrase next to another that refers to the same thing: *We'll take the easiest route, **the east ridge,** to the top*. The word or phrase in apposition is marked off from the thing to which it refers by a pair of commas.

appraise *or* **apprise** To **appraise** is to evaluate or assess: *The project was appraised as being viable.* To **apprise** is to inform: *We were apprised of the committee's decision.* Be especially careful not to write *appraised of*.

appurtenance Spelling: remember the **ur**.

apt See ◊liable.

aqueduct Spelling: note the **e** (not **a**) in the middle.

Arab, Arabian, *or* **Arabic** As adjectives, **Arab** is used mainly of the Arabs and their modern countries, **Arabian** of Arabia (the peninsula between the Red Sea and the Persian Gulf), and **Arabic** of the languages and literature of the Arabs: *The Arab nations now include countries outside the natural limits of the Arabian Peninsula, and the Arabic language has adopted many forms in those countries.*

archetypal Spelling: remember the **e** in the middle, not an **i**.

arctic The **c** in the middle of this word should be pronounced and should not be forgotten when the word is spelled.

aristocrat The standard British pronunciation is with the stress on the first syllable. The beginning of the word rhymes with **Harry**. Americans stress the second syllable [er-**wrist**-tercrat].

arrogate See ◊abdicate.

artefact *or* **artifact** This word can be spelled either way.

article In grammar, this is a part of speech. There are two articles in English: the definite article **the** and the indefinite article **a** or **an**. The definite article identifies a particular noun: *the book I need* and the indefinite article indicates an unidentified noun: *bring me a book*. The indefinite article *an* is used in front of a vowel: *an owl*.

artifact See ◊artefact.

artisan The main British pronunciation is with the stress on the last syllable. Americans and some British speakers stress the first syllable.

artist *or* **artiste** An **artist** is anyone engaged in the fine or performing arts, such as a painter, sculptor, actor, or entertainer: *Les Dawson was a popular pantomime artist*. An **artiste** is usually a singer or dancer, or else a person skilled in a special craft: *The hotel chef has trained professionally and is a real artiste*.

as See ◊like.

as ... as *There is in Georgia a mafia as powerful as or even more powerful than the Sicilian one*. It is quite common, especially in spoken English, to leave out the second **as** in sentences like this: *There is in Georgia a mafia as powerful or even more powerful than the Sicilian one*. But this is not regarded as acceptable in standard English. Keep the second *as*.

This construction can sound rather stilted or awkward. If you want to avoid it, you can switch the sentence around, like this: *There is in Georgia a mafia as powerful as the Sicilian one, or even more powerful*.

It is perfectly acceptable in colloquial English to leave out the first of a pair of *as*s in comparisons: *I was (as) pleased as Punch to get the job*.

ascetic See ◊aesthetic.

Asian *or* **Asiatic** The terms were at one time interchangeable for anyone or anything from Asia. **Asian** is now generally applied to people and their languages: *He has an Asian girlfriend*, and **Asiatic** to things: *The Asiatic plains and deserts are awesome in their vastness*.

A British person referring to an Asian will probably mean someone from the Indian sub-continent, or whose ancestors came from there. An American will probably mean someone whose roots lie further east, in the area between the Indian and Pacific Oceans (the Vietnamese, Koreans, Thais, Japanese, etc). See also ◊Indian.

asinine Spelling: remember the single s.

asphalt The first syllable is *as*, not *ash*, and is pronounced like the **a** at the beginning of *apple*. Some people pronounce *phalt* as [felt], but this is not standard. Spelling: remember there is no **h** before the **p**.

assassin Spelling: remember the two double ss.

assiduous Spelling: remember the double s.

assimilate Spelling: remember the two ss and one **m**.

assonance Spelling: remember the double s and single **n**.

assuage See ◊allay.

assure, ensure, *or* **insure** To **assure** something is to make certain it will happen: *Victory is assured for the younger, fitter boxer as he has the advantage.* To **ensure** something is to take steps to make sure that something happens: *Seat belts should ensure that you will be unhurt in an accident.* To **insure** something is to take precautions against something undesirable happening: *The concertgoers insured against disappointment by buying their tickets early.*

asthma Spelling: remember the **th**.

atheist See ◊agnostic.

atrophy The stress is on the first syllable, and the word is pronounced [**at**-ruh-fee]. Note that the end of the word is pronounced [fee], not [fie].

attach Spelling: note the ending **-ch**, not **-tch**.

attenuate Spelling: remember the double **t** and single **n**.

aural *or* **oral** Anything **aural** relates to the ear and so to hearing: *The doctor arranged an aural examination for his patient; Many teachers work with both aural and written material.* Anything **oral** relates to the mouth and so to speaking: *The French exam was in two parts: first written, then oral; Many of the stories were passed down by oral tradition, and had never been written down before.*

autumn Spelling: remember the **mn**.

auxiliary Spelling: note there is only one **l**.

auxiliary verb A verb that, when used with other verbs, expresses a particular grammatical function or meaning. In the sentences *I might have attended; You must have known; You do see; That can be arranged,* the auxiliary verbs are: *might have, must have, do,* and *can be.*

averse *or* **adverse** A person who is **averse** to something does not like it or is not keen on it: *Are you averse to shopping?; He's not averse to a tipple now and then.* A thing that is **adverse** to someone or something is hostile or harmful to them: *Many campaigners saw the election result as adverse to the cause of democracy.*

avow *or* **vouch** To **avow** something is to admit or declare it publicly: *He avowed his determination to get his own back*; *She avowed herself to be a loyal supporter of the party*. To **vouch** for someone or something is to produce evidence in support of them: *I can vouch for her honesty*; *Can you vouch for the truth of that?*

awake, awaken, wake, *or* **waken** All these mean to cease sleeping, or to rouse someone from sleep. In everyday speech **wake** or **wake up** are used: *I usually wake early, but today my mother woke me up at noon.* **Awake** can be used in speech, but is more common in writing. *Wake up* is the usual form when giving an order: *Go and wake your father up*; *Dad, wake up! Awake* is sometimes used in literature and poetry: *'Awake, beloved, for the new day dawns!'*

    Awaken and **waken** are slightly old-fashioned words, used in writing, usually meaning 'rouse someone from sleep': *He crept in, trying not to waken his wife*; *She was awakened by the sound of the door opening.* Note the difference in the tenses of these verbs: *Wake* has the past tense *woke* and past participle *woken. Awake* is similar: *she awakes, she awoke, she has awoken.* The past tense and past participle of *waken* is *wakened. Awakened* is similar: *he awakens, he awakened, he has awakened.*

axe US spelling: *ax*.

bachelor Spelling: note that there is no **t**.

bail *or* **bale** To **bail** someone out is to provide cash to get them out of prison, or more generally to help them out of a difficult situation, especially a financial one: *I had to borrow £500 to bail John out*; *If you hadn't bailed me out last year I don't know what I would have done*. To **bail** water out is to scoop it out with a bucket or other container: *We bailed out the water that was coming into the boat*. To **bale** out is to jump from an aircraft: *The pilot had to bale out when the engine failed*. However, **bail** is also used in this last sense, especially in the US: *The pilot bailed out*.

baited See ◊bated.

bale See ◊bail.

balk *or* **baulk** This word can be spelled either way.

balloon Spelling: remember the double **l** and double **o**.

balmy *or* **barmy** Remember that **balmy** means pleasant or soothing, and **barmy** means mad.

baluster See ◊banister.

banal The word is pronounced with the stress on the second syllable [buh-**narl**]. The first syllable is the same as the first syllable of *banana*.

banister *or* **baluster** A **banister** is one of the upright rails supporting the handrail in a staircase: *Most children like to slide down the banisters if they get a chance*. A **baluster** is one of the short pillars supporting the rail or stone coping round a balcony, terrace or the like: *Many balusters are narrow at the top and bottom and swell out in the middle*.

bankruptcy Spelling: remember the **t**.

basically This can be used to introduce a simplified explanation containing only the most essential point: *It's basically a matter of finance* (although there is more to it than just a lack of money). It is often used as a meaningless filler: *Basically, I'm going tomorrow*. This is best avoided.

bated *or* **baited** Bated is related to abated, so means 'lessened': *We waited with bated breath to see who had won.* **Baited** means 'enticed' or 'tormented': *The mousetrap was baited with cheese*; *The class baited the new teacher, trying to make him lose his temper.*

battalion Spelling: remember the double **t**, as in *battle*, and a single **l**.

baulk See ◁balk.

beautiful Spelling: remember the **eau**.

becomes See ◁behoves.

beg the question This is often used to mean 'evade the question', 'avoid giving a straight answer'. It actually means to assume the truth of something which has yet to be proved, and to base a conclusion on this assumption, evading the question in the sense of failing to ask rather than failing to answer.

beginning Spelling: remember the one **g** and two **ns**.

behalf To act or speak **on behalf of** someone or **on** someone's **behalf** is to do so as their representative. *On behalf of* should not be confused with *on the part of*: a speech *on behalf of* the Chairman is made by someone else, expressing the Chairman's thoughts: a speech *on the part of* the Chairman is one he makes himself.

In American English *behalf* is also used with *in*, to mean 'in someone's interest', 'for someone's benefit': *Several people argued in his behalf.*

behoves *or* **becomes** Behoves, always preceded by *it*, is used of something that is right or necessary: *It ill behoves you to speak thus of your grandparents* (you should not speak of them like that). **Becomes** is used of something that is fitting, appropriate or (especially of clothes) well suited: *It ill becomes you to speak thus of your grandparents* (it is not the sort of way I expect you to speak about them); *Amanda's new outfit certainly becomes her.*

beleaguered Spelling: note the **ue** after the **g**.

believe Spelling: remember the **ie**.

benefited Spelling: note the single **t**, which is because the syllable is unstressed.

bequeath Spelling: note there is no **e** on the end.

bereaved *or* **bereft** The words are related, but are now used in quite distinct senses. **Bereaved** is used of a person who has been deprived of someone, often a relative, through their death: *The bereaved family are still in a state of shock*. **Bereft** is used of a person who has been deprived of anything at all: *I was quite bereft of speech* (I couldn't speak); *'Of friends, of hope, of all bereft'* (William Cowper).

berserk Spelling: remember the first **r**.

beseige Spelling: note this is an exception to the rule *i before e except after c*.

beside *or* **besides** Beside means next to: *There was no one beside Jane* (there was no one next to her). **Besides** means in addition to: *There was no one besides Jane* (she was the only one there).

between *or* **among** Among is usually preferred to **between** when more than two parties are involved: *The money is to be divided between the two brothers, or among their descendants*. However, *between* is used when speaking about a relationship involving two or more parties: *a contest between Britain, France and Germany*. It is also used when describing the position of something: *The house lies between the motorway, the factory and the railway*.

between you and me *Between you and me* is acceptable in standard English; *between you and I* isn't. This is because *between* is a preposition, and pronouns that come after prepositions are in the accusative case (here, *me*), not the nominative case (not *I*).

The same applies to a pair of pronouns that is the object of a verb: *They've invited you and me to dinner* is acceptable, *They've invited you and I to dinner* isn't.

The reason why expressions like *between you and I* have become so common is that people are aware that the accusative case is not correct for the subject of a verb (*You and I have been invited* is acceptable; *You and me have been invited* is not), so they make the mistake of thinking it is not correct anywhere, and always use the nominative case.

If you are in any doubt, try leaving out the first pronoun of the pair. That will show you what case the second one should be: *between I* and *they've invited I* are clearly ungrammatical.

biannual *or* **biennial** A **biannual** event happens twice a year: *We make a biannual visit to the in-laws: once at Christmas and again in the summer*. A **biennial** event happens every two years: *The school was due for its biennial inspection*. (A *biennial* plant lasts two years.)

biased *or* **biassed** This word can be spelled either way.

bicycle Spelling: remember it as **bi** (meaning 'two') plus **cycle**.

biennial See ▷biannual.

bilious Spelling: note the single **l**, as in *bile*.

billion In British English *billion* has traditionally meant a million million. The American meaning of *billion* (a thousand million) has become standard in technical and financial use, and it is now better to use it in all circumstances.

biscuit Spelling: remember the **ui**.

bisect See ▷dissect.

bi-weekly, bi-monthly Bi-weekly can mean either 'every other week' or 'twice a week'. The same problem arises with **bi-monthly**. The only way to avoid the ambiguity is not to use the words at all.

bizarre Spelling: note the single **z** and double **r**.

black Black is the term preferred by most black people. *Negro* is disliked by many, and *Negress* is felt to be particularly insulting, especially by American blacks. *Coloured*, as a term for all people who are not white, should also be avoided, as most black and brown people dislike it; *nonwhite* is acceptable.

blanch See ▷blench.

blasé The British pronunciation has the stress on the first syllable [**blah**-zay] but the US pronunciation has the stress on the second syllable.

blatant *or* **flagrant** A **blatant** offence or injustice is a glaring or obvious one: *She said she was out, but that's a blatant lie as I saw her through the window*. A **flagrant** offence is similar but stronger, implying a deliberate flouting of a law or code of behaviour: *The judge's verdict was thought to be a flagrant miscarriage of justice.*

blench *or* **blanch** To **blench** is to go pale through fear or some strong emotion: *The nurse blenched when she saw the first victim*. To **blanch** is similar, but is often used of the part of the body that turns pale: *His cheeks blanched in horror.*

blond *or* **blonde** Spelling: use **blond** if you are writing about a boy or a man, and **blonde** if writing about a girl or a woman.

bludgeon Spelling: remember the **d** before the **g**.

bolero This word has two pronunciations. A [**boll**-uh-roe] is the short sleeveless jacket worn by Spanish dancers, and a [bull-**air**-roe] is the Spanish dance or music.

bona fide The phrase is pronounced [boner-fie-dee].

born *or* **borne** Both verbs derive from a verb *bear*. **Born** relates to giving birth: *She was born in August*. **Borne** relates to any other kind of carrying or bearing: *The seeds of the dandelion are borne by the wind*; *He died yesterday after an illness bravely borne*; *It was borne in on me how close they had been together*.

bourgeois Spelling: remember especially the **e** after the **g**.

bracket This is another word for parenthesis. Brackets separate a word or phrase from the rest of the sentence. You can use them to add information without breaking up the main sentence, which still remains intact if the words in the brackets are removed: *How could Jim (a man he had known for years) behave towards him in such a despicable manner?* The information in brackets is not crucial to the structure and meaning of the sentence.

   A pair of commas can be used in the same way as brackets when the subsidiary piece of information has a stronger link with the main sentence; for example: *The horses, which had been toiling all morning, were given an hour's break at noon.* A pair of dashes can also be used parenthetically. See also ⏵dash.

breach *or* **breech** **Breach** relates to *break* in some sense: *It was clear there had been a serious breach of confidence*; *The tank made a breach in the wall*. **Breech** relates to the lower or bottom part of someone or something: *The baby was born by a breech delivery* (feet or buttocks first, instead of head first, as more usual).

Britain, Great Britain, United Kingdom, British Isles
Britain or **Great Britain** refers to the island comprising England, Scotland, and Wales, with the small adjacent islands. **Britain** is also used as a historical term, referring to these islands before the coming of the Anglo-Saxons. **United Kingdom** is short for 'The United Kingdom of Great Britain and Northern Ireland'. Between 1801, when Great Britain and Ireland were united, and 1920, when Ireland was partitioned, *United Kingdom* also included southern Ireland, now the Republic of Ireland. **British Isles** refers to the island group which includes Great Britain and Ireland; it is a geographical term, not a political one. Natives

or citizens of the United Kingdom are officially *British*, although they may describe themselves as *English*, *Irish*, *Scots*, or *Welsh*. See also ◊England.

Brittany Spelling: note the double **t**, unlike *Britain*.

broach *or* **brooch** Remember that to **broach** something is to open or introduce it, whereas a **brooch** is an ornament.

broccoli Spelling: note the two **c**s and one **l**.

brooch See ◊broach.

Buddha Spelling: note the double **d**.

budgeted Spelling: note the single **t**.

bulrush Spelling: note the single **l**.

buoy This word (as in *life buoy*) is easy to misspell. Remember the **u**. Related words are *buoyant* and *buoyancy*.

bureaucracy Spelling: note the **eau**.

bursar Spelling: note the ending **-ar**, not **-er**.

business *or* **busyness** Business is the doing or carrying out of something: *He made it his business to find out*; *It is the business of the local council to provide public services*. **Busyness** is the state of being busy: *The squirrel is well known for its busyness: it is always bustling about*.

C

caddie *or* **caddy** Caddie is the usual spelling in golf, although **caddy** may also be used, both as a noun and a verb. A *caddy* is a box for storing tea.

cajole Spelling: note there is no **d** before the **j**.

calendar Spelling: note the single **l**, and the ending **-ar**.

calibre Spelling: note the single **l**. US spelling: **caliber**.

callipers Spelling: note the double **l** and single **p**. US spelling: *calipers*.

callous *or* **callus** The words are related in their common derivation from Latin *callum*, meaning 'hardened skin'. **Callous** is an adjective, meaning 'hard' in the sense of being cruelly insensitive: *He gave a callous laugh*. **Callus** is a noun which is a term for an area of hard skin on the feet or hands.

camaraderie Spelling: note the **a** after the **m**, not an **e**.

camellia Spelling: note the single **m** and double **l**.

camouflage Spelling: note the single **m**.

can *or* **may** There is still some controversy over the use of these words. Both **can** and **may** express the idea of giving or requesting permission: *Can I come in? May I come in?* This use of *can* is comparatively recent (it is first recorded in the 1870s), but over the past hundred years or so it has decidedly overtaken *may*, and now it is a perfectly normal part of standard English.

There are rare cases where the use of *can* creates genuine ambiguity. When *can* can in theory mean either 'be able to' or 'be allowed to' (as in *What if she asks me what he can do?*), in practice the context usually makes it clear which is meant.

There is always the option of using *may* instead, but remember that even in questions it sounds quite formal: *May I come in?* In positive and negative sentences its natural habitat is official pronouncements: *Persons under 16 may not use this facility.*

However, **may** is more often the cause of real ambiguity than *can*: does *They may not go until Thursday* mean that they are not allowed to go, or that it is possible that they will not go?

candelabra Spelling: note the **el**, not **le** as in *candle.*

canon *or* **cannon** Both words are related to *cane*. The use of a cane as a measuring rod gave **canon** in the sense of 'rule', 'standard', and from that the sense of 'priest' (who lives under a church rule). The cane as a tube gave **cannon** as a gun or piece of artillery. The word takes no plural **s**: *'Cannon to right of them,/Cannon to left of them,/Cannon in front of them/Volley'd and thunder'd'* (Tennyson).

canvas *or* **canvass** The words have a common origin but have developed quite different senses. **Canvas** is both the coarse cloth used for making tents and sails and also the cloth that artists paint on: *His canvas gradually became a painting of a sailing boat under full canvas.* To **canvass** is to solicit support from voters before an election: *On the eve of the election the party workers went out canvassing.*

capital *or* **capitol** A **capital** is the town or city that is a country's seat of government: *Berlin is now again the capital of Germany.* A **capitol** is a statehouse in the USA, i.e. the building that houses a state's legislature: *One of the USA's best known buildings is the Capitol, the meeting place of the Congress of the United States of America in Washington, DC, the US capital.*

capital letter This is an upper-case letter; see ◊case, upper and lower.

capitol See ◊capital.

carat *or* **karat** This word (meaning a unit of weight, especially a unit for measuring gold) can be spelled either way.

carcase *or* **carcass** This word can be spelled either way but American English uses only *carcass*.

career *or* **careen** To **career** is to go rapidly and even dangerously: *I held the strap tight as the taxi careered down the steep hill.* To **careen** is to sway or tilt dangerously to one side: *The amusement park train careened first to one side then to the other as it hurtled round the track.*

Caribbean When British people talk about the *Caribbean* the word is usually pronounced [carry-**bee**-yun] but in expressions such as *Caribbean island* the main stress shifts back on to the first syllable. A few speakers always pronounce the word [k'**rib**-ian]. The US pronunciation is [ke-**rib**-ian].

Spelling: remember the single **r** and double **b**.

caricature Spelling: note that there is no **h** after the first **c**.

carp See ◊cavil.

cartilage Spelling: note the single **l** and the ending **-age**, not **-ege**.

case in grammar, case indicates the differing functions of nouns and pronouns in their sentences. In English, six pronouns have one form when they are the subject of the verb, and a different form when they are either objects of the verb or governed by a preposition. The six are: *I/me, he/him, she/her, we/us, they/them, who/whom*. See ◊accusative, nominative.

case, upper and lower These are the two possible forms taken by letters of the alphabet in typescript: capital letters (upper case) and small letters (lower case). Capitals are used to begin proper nouns: *John; Concorde; Dr Smith*; at the beginning of a sentence: *The cat sat on the mat*; at the beginning of a sentence of direct speech: *He said: 'Come here!'*); and for the principal words in a title: *Far from the Madding Crowd*.

In the days when typesetting was done by hand, printers used to keep letters in a low case, near to hand; the less often used capitals were stored in a higher (upper) case.

cassette Spelling: remember that it has double **s** and double **t**.

caster *or* **castor** As applied to the sugar sprinkler and the swivelling wheel on furniture, the words can have either spelling: *Caster sugar is finely ground white sugar*; *It can be difficult to move a bed if it is not on castors*. *Castor oil*, however, has only the one spelling.

catalyst A **catalyst** is a substance which encourages chemical changes in other substances without being changed itself. The word is often used figuratively to mean something or someone that precipitates change without being directly involved in it: *The war was a catalyst for social change*. It should not be used simply to mean 'cause'.

catarrh Spelling: remember the **rrh**, as in *haemorrhage* and *diarrhoea*.

catch 22 This refers to a predicament from which there is no escape because of conditions which contradict or exclude each other. It comes from Joseph Heller's novel *Catch 22* in which a bomber pilot pretends to be insane so that he will be grounded, but his wish to avoid danger shows his sanity.

catechism Spelling: note the single **t**, and no **r** after the **e**.

caterpillar Spelling: remember the one **t** and two **l**s.

catholic *or* **Catholic** With a small letter, **catholic** is used of something general or universal: *She has very catholic tastes*. With a capital letter, it refers to the Roman Catholic Church: *The Catholic population is smaller than the Protestant*. Even in a religious context, and with a capital letter (as used in a former style of English), *Catholic* may still mean universal: *'And I believe one Catholick and Apostolic Church'* (Book of Common Prayer: Nicene Creed).

caviare *or* **caviar** This word can be spelled either way.

cavil *or* **carp** To **cavil** is to raise irritating or trivial objections: *He cavilled when I proposed a trip to London, saying the journey bored him*. To **carp** is to find fault, often pettily and unreasonably: *The music critic carped at the conductor's flamboyant style*.

ceiling Spelling: note the **ei**.

cemetery Spelling: remember there are three **e**s.

censor *or* **censure** To **censor** something is to ban or suppress it, often on moral grounds: *The publisher censored part of the play because of its bad language*. To **censure** something is to criticize it or find fault with it: *The tennis player was censured for his unsporting behaviour on court*.

centre around Some people still maintain that **centre**, when it is used figuratively to mean 'be concentrated in', 'be taken up by', should be followed only by **on** or **in**: *Her interests are centred on her career*. However, *centre round* or *around* have been in use for many years and there is no reason to avoid them; if you wish to, use *revolve*: *His whole life revolves around football*.

centrifugal British speakers say mainly [sentry-**phew**-gle] when the adjective stands alone and is not followed by a noun: *It's centrifugal*, but they shift the main stress on to the first syllable [**sen**-trif-yougle] if the word comes before a noun: *centrifugal force*. The US pronunciation is [sen-**trif**-yer-gle].

ceremonial *or* **ceremonious** If something is **ceremonial** it is proper for a ceremony: *The victory was marked by a ceremonial parade*; *The best china was brought out only on ceremonial occasions*. If it is

ceremonious it is done with great ceremony, that is, extremely politely or formally: *He gave my wife a ceremonious bow, as if she were a princess.*

cervical The pronunciation [sir-**vy**-kle] is the one mainly used in British English, but [**sir**-vickle] is also used. The US pronunciation has the stress on the first syllable.

chafe *or* **chaff** To **chafe** is to irritate or be annoyed: *Nancy's shoes were chafing*; *The passengers were chafing at the long delay.* To **chaff** someone is to tease them: *The trainee was chaffed about his girlish locks.* **Chaff** is also the husks that are separated from seeds during threshing.

chair(person) Formerly anyone, male or female, who took the chair at a meeting was called the *chairman.* Some people did not like this, and invented *chairwoman* for a female, and *chairperson* or *chair* for either sex. There is now no generally accepted term, and the usage depends very much on the feelings of the participants. A woman chairing a meeting may still be correctly addressed as *Madam Chairman* if she does not object (she may prefer it to the alternative *Madam Chair*). *Mr* or *Madam Chairperson* and *Mr Chair* are not generally used as forms of address, although there is no logical reason to avoid them.

chamois With the meaning 'wash leather' this word is pronounced [**shammy**], but with the 'animal' meaning (a kind of goat antelope) it is pronounced [**sham**-wah], more like the French original.

changeable Spelling: remember that the **e** of *change* remains.

charade The standard British pronunciation is [shuh-**rard**]. The US pronunciation [shuh-**raid**] is sometimes heard in Britain.

cheque US spelling: *check.*

chilblain Spelling: note the single **l**.

chilli (pepper) US spelling: *chili.* Do not confuse it with the name of the South American country, *Chile.*

chiropodist The recommended British pronunciation is [ki-**rop**-uhdist] with a **k** sound at the beginning. The US pronunciation is similar. In Britain a pronunciation beginning with **sh** is also heard.

chivy *or* **chivvy** This word can be spelled either way.

cholesterol Spelling: remember the **h**.

chord See ◊cord.

chrysalis Spelling: remember the **h**.

cinnamon Spelling: note the double **n**.

cipher *or* **cypher** This word can be spelled either way.

circumstances *under the circumstances* is well-established and quite acceptable, although it is sometimes objected to because *circumstance* comes from the Latin *circum*, meaning 'around'. Some people prefer to use **in the circumstances** to indicate a simple state of affairs and **under the circumstances** when the circumstances compel someone to do something, but there is no real need to make this distinction. *In* or *under* can be used in (or under) any circumstances.

cirrhosis Spelling: note the **rrh** as in *catarrh*.

civil, civic, *or* **civilian** Civil relates to a citizen, with all that it implies: *It is your civil duty to protect your neighbours*. **Civic** relates to a city, as well as its citizens: *The town's local government offices are at the Civic Centre*. **Civilian** is used of someone or something that is not military: *Civilian life is not always easier than life in the army*. *Civil* also has the non-military sense, and is used of something non-legal or non-ecclesiastical: *They didn't get married in church but had a civil ceremony in a registry office*. *Civil* can also mean 'polite'.

claim Be careful when using *claim* to mean 'say', 'state', or 'declare'. The primary meaning of *claim* is to demand something that you are entitled to or to assert your right to it, in this case the right to be believed, and it implies that you may not be. *He said he had been burgled* is neutral: there is no reason to question the statement. *He claimed he had been burgled* suggests that he may not be telling the truth.

clandestine The standard pronunciation is with the stress on the second syllable [clan-**dess**-tin] but many people stress the word on the first syllable [**clan**-dess-tine] or [**clan**-dess-tin].

classic *or* **classical** Something is **classic** if it is the first or finest of its kind, or is regarded as standard: *This book is the classic authority on bee-keeping*. **Classical** also has this sense, but implies a link with the culture of Greece and Rome: *The statue had a classical simplicity and beauty*.

clause is a part of a sentence that contains a subject and a verb, and is joined to the rest of the sentence by a conjunction. In English, if the conjunction is *and, but*, or *or*, the clause is a coordinating clause; with any other conjunction it is a subordinating clause.

claustrophobia Spelling: remember **au** first, and then **o**.

clayey Spelling: note the ending **-yey**.

clematis The standard British pronunciation is with the stress on the first syllable and with a weak second syllable [**clem**-uhtiss]. However, [cluh-**may**-tiss] is also heard. The US pronunciation is [**clem**-ertus].

clichés, pretentious language, and jargon

These are three kinds of language to avoid. Some expressions belong to more than one category.

1. Clichés

Clichés are words and phrases that were once fashionable, but that have been overused and used inappropriately and mindlessly to the point that they mean very little. Many people have grown tired of them, and see their continued use by others as a sign that they have little to say.

Most clichés are phrases rather than individual words, that is, they are prefabricated pieces of language rather than words put together by the user. Lazy writers and speakers use them as lazy cooks use ready meals from the supermarket, and they are just as unappetizing. The occasional cliché does no harm if used appropriately. Indeed, they can be a useful short cut in communication, but a text in which cliché follows cliché will seem very stale. Here are some to avoid:

according to plan
at this moment in time
auspicious occasion
blot on the landscape
the bottom line
when the chips are down
when it comes to the crunch
conventional wisdom
cutting edge
crisis of confidence
at the end of the day
fundamentally flawed
give something a clean bill of
   health
golden opportunity
in the last analysis
in this day and age
key player
leading edge
level playing-field
life-style
light years

literally
meaningful
move the goalposts
the nitty-gritty
on the table
overkill
player (*a major player on the
   world stage*)
put in place
put on the back burner
put on hold
quantum leap
splendid isolation
Tell me about it!
the tip of the iceberg
until such time as
up front
up and running
vibrant
a whole new ballgame
a wide range of issues
You tell me!

2. Pretentious language

Overlapping with clichés, another kind of language to be avoided is pretentious language, in which the choice of words tends to make the user and the user's subject appear more important. If other people recognize what is going on, this kind of language can backfire. Here are some examples:

address a problem
communicate something to somebody (tell them)
concessionary rates
consigned to oblivion
differential (difference)
-driven (event-driven; quality-driven)
escalate (increase)
event (*craft event, performance event*)
experience (*The White Cliffs experience*)
facility (*leisure facility*)
in-depth (*an in-depth study*)
in terms of
in the event of (if there is)
mandate
ongoing
operational
pro-active
simplistic
situation (*an ongoing fire situation*)
state-of-the-art
take cognizance of (*We will be taking cognizance of what our members say*)
terminate
thereby
utilize (use)

Job advertisements are a good place to see examples of pretentious language.

In all these posts we are looking for high-calibre, technically excellent individuals who can knit closely together, combining their skills, knowledge and experience in a dynamic start-up environment.

...a solutions-driven approach and in-depth knowledge
...create a culture of growth which permeates throughout the operation, primarily to the shop based sales staff.

3. Jargon

Pretentious language in its turn overlaps with jargon. Words and phrases that start life in a particular subject area may be taken up by outsiders. These outsiders may use them as vivid and effective labels for things in other fields, or simply as terms meant to impress upon others that their users are up-to-date and sophisticated, and know more than the people they are addressing.

Track record from athletics is an example. If we look again at job advertisements, we find *proven track record*, a piece of jargon that is long-winded, and has become a cliché. Here are some more examples of jargon:

agree a deal	matrix
catalyst	oriented
come on stream	orientated
environment (= conditions)	parameter
input	scenario (*worst case scenario*)
interface	traumatic
logistics	user-friendly

Many specialist terms are pretentious jargon from the start. Does a *human resources manager* really need to ask that a sales director be *results orientated*? Will the new appointee really prefer a *rewards package* to the salary with other benefits that he had in his previous company?

See also ◊plain English, ◊legalese, ◊officialese, and entries at ◊actually, ◊basically, ◊commence, ◊interface, ◊key, ◊parameter, and ◊situation.

climax Climax comes from a Greek word meaning 'ladder' and as a technical term in rhetoric means the arrangement of ideas in a series in which each is more impressive than the one before. In general use it means 'a culmination', 'a peak of intensity'. Some people disapprove of *climax* used as a verb meaning 'come' or 'bring to a climax', but this is now well-established and there is no good reason to avoid it.

cluster Spelling: note the ending -**er**, not -**re**.

coccyx Spelling: note the **ccy** in the middle.

coconut Spelling: remember that there is no **a** in the middle.

cocoon Spelling: note the single **c** in the middle.

colander Spelling: note the **o**, and the ending **-er**.

collateral Spelling: note the double **l**.

collective nouns A collective noun, or group noun, is a noun which designates a group of people or animals. *Crew, committee, gang, government, audience, family*, and *herd* are all collective nouns.

When such a group is considered as a single unit, its collective noun is used with a singular verb and singular pronouns: *The committee has reached its decision*. But when the focus is on the individual members of the group, British English tends to use a plural verb and plural pronouns with its collective nouns: *The committee have been arguing all morning over what they should do*. American English usually uses a singular verb and pronouns in these circumstances.

A determiner in front of a singular collective noun is always singular: *this committee*, never *these committee* (but of course when the collective noun is pluralized, it takes a plural determiner: *these committees*).

colon This is a punctuation mark (:) commonly used before a direct quotation: *She said: 'Leave it out.'* or a list, or to add detail to a statement: *That is his cat: the fluffy white one*.

colonnade Spelling: note the single **l** and double **n**.

coloration Spelling: remember that there is no **u** before the **r**.

colossal Spelling: note the single **l** and double **s**.

colosseum Spelling: note the single **l** and double **s**. An alternative spelling is *coliseum*.

coloured See ◊black.

comic *or* **comical** Comic is used of something intended to be amusing (though it may not be): *Phil then sang one of his comic songs*. **Comical** is used of something amusing (though not necessarily intended to be): *The toddler pulled a comical face when he dropped his mug*.

comma This is a punctuation mark (,) most commonly used to mark off a phrase or noun in apposition: *Billy, the last man, did not let us down*, mark off a subordinate clause or phrase: *Old Mrs Parsons, who had lived there all her life, could not remember such a thing happening before*, or separate items in a list: *The box was full of nails, screws, pins, string, and tape*.

Commas are also used to mark off sentence connectors such as *however, nevertheless, moreover*: *Nevertheless, I can say, without any doubt, that he deserved his success*. There are other occasions where a comma is needed to indicate a pause or a slight change of direction in the sentence. For example, *I certainly won't see him again, although I can't help liking him*. Commas are often incorrectly used where a stronger stop is required: *We saw John last night, it was good to see him again*. Although the meaning is clear, the use of a comma here is grammatically incorrect. A full stop or semicolon should be used.

commemorate Spelling: note the double **m** first, then a single **m**.

commence Commence is a formal word for 'start' or 'begin'. It is not generally used in conversation, and looks pompous in all but the most formal writing.

commiserate Spelling: note the two **ms** and one **s**.

committee Spelling: remember the three double letters **m**, **t**, and **e**.

common See ▷mutual.

communal The preferred British pronunciation is [**kom**-yer-nal] with the stress on the first syllable, but some people say [ker-**myoo**-nal]. This is also the US pronunciation.

comparable The preferred British pronunciation is with the stress on the first syllable and with a weak second syllable [**com**-prable]. A pronunciation that starts with a weak syllable and then sounds the same as *parable* is also heard. The US pronunciation is [**carm**-prable].

comparative The form of an adjective usually ending in *-er*, indicating the greater of two qualities being compared. For example, *she is older, wiser and happier than her brother*. The comparative of some adjectives is formed by preceding them with *more* instead of the *-er* ending: *He is more beautiful and more generous than his sister*. See also ▷superlative. Spelling: note the second **a**.

compare *Compare* is used with *to* to suggest similarity: *She compared him to* (she said he was like) *a knight in shining armour*. Followed by *and, with,* or a plural, *compare* refers to an analysis of similarities and differences: *Compare Shakespeare's* Antony and Cleopatra *and Shaw's* Caesar and Cleopatra; *The Ford Escort was compared with other cars in the same price range; a survey comparing opinions about smoking*. If it is used without an object, meaning 'compete' or 'be compared with', *compare* is followed by *with*: *Tinned strawberries can't compare with fresh ones*. *Compared* can be followed by *to* or *with*: *Compared to* (or *with*) *her, I'm a genius*.

competent Spelling: remember the two es.

competition Spelling: remember it has **ti** twice.

complacent, complaisant, *or* **compliant** Complacent refers to a feeling of self-satisfaction: *Grace left for home with a complacent smile: she knew she had done a good day's work*. **Complaisant** refers to a willingness to comply or oblige: *'The girl was complaisant enough to make the bearers stop'* (Jonathan Swift). **Compliant** refers to an actual complying or obliging, whether willingly or not: *All the courtiers were compliant with the royal will*.

complaisant See ⍙complacent.

complement In grammar, a word or phrase that follows the verb and tells us about the subject: *John was **an accountant**; Jane appeared **bored***. Noun and adjective complements follow verbs such as *to be, to seem, to become*.

complement *or* **compliment** To **complement** something is to suit it or complete it: *That shirt complements your suit nicely*. To **compliment** someone is to praise them or approve of them: *She complimented the child on his good manners*. If you think of the first five letters of *complete* when you are trying to spell *complement*, it will help you spell these two words correctly.

compliant See ⍙complacent.

compliment See ⍙complement.

compose See ⍙consist.

compound subject A compound subject, or coordinate subject, consists of two or more nouns or pronouns joined by a conjunction or preposition, which together form the subject of a single verb. It can be difficult to decide whether this verb should be singular or plural.

If the nouns or pronouns are joined by *and*, the verb is usually plural: *My mother and I are going to Weston-super-Mare for our holidays*. This applies even if one of the nouns is omitted: *Both red wine and white are made in the area*. But when the two nouns refer to the same person or thing, the verb is singular: *My flatmate, and fellow team member, has broken his leg*. And when the two linked nouns have become a fixed phrase, representing a single entity, the verb is singular: *Fish and chips is all he ever eats*.

If the nouns or pronouns are joined by *or* or *nor* (usually preceded by *either* or *neither*), the verb depends on the nouns or pronouns themselves. If both are singular, the verb is singular: *The guard or his assistant has locked the gate*. If both are plural, the verb is plural: *Neither the Americans nor the Russians want this policy to succeed*. If one is singular and one is plural, the verb agrees with the noun or pronoun closest to it: *Either the twins or Bob is going to come round to help you; Neither the time nor the resources are available*. If the two pronouns conflict in person, the verb should agree with the second pronoun: *Either you or I am likely to be chosen*. But this usually sounds awkward, and it is probably better to rewrite the sentence to avoid the choice: *Either you or I will probably be chosen*.

If the nouns or pronouns are joined by prepositions such as *as well as; in addition to; rather than; with*, the verb is singular: *Determination as well as skill is needed in this job*.

compound word Two or more words linked to create a new one: *boyfriend*; *long-winded*; *motorbike*; *meeting room*. The two words can be merged, separated by a space, or hyphenated.

comprise See ▷consist.

compulsive, impulsive, *or* impetuous A **compulsive** action is one done involuntarily: *He was so nervous that he gave a compulsive laugh whenever she spoke to him*. An **impulsive** action is one done on the spur of the moment, without hesitation, often as a consequence of a 'gut feeling' that it is right: *She gave him an impulsive kiss*. An **impetuous** action is a rash or impulsive one, often performed with some vigour: *He gave an impetuous flick of his hand to motion the beggar away*.

concede See ▷accede.

concise Spelling: remember the **c** in the middle, not **s**.

conditional clause In a sentence, a clause where the action proposed in the main clause is dependent on the fulfilment of the subordinate clause: *If you are good, you can go to the party; You can't go unless you have a ticket*.

Conditional clauses are introduced by the conjunctions *if* or *unless*.

condole *or* console To **condole** with somebody is to express sympathy with them; to **console** someone is to give them sympathy or comfort them: *When her mother died, I first condoled with her on her loss then did my best to console her*.

condone This means to overlook or forgive bad behaviour, or to treat it as unimportant; a woman is said to condone her husband's adultery if she

continues to live with him as his wife although she knows what is going
on. It can be used to mean 'agree to' (perhaps reluctantly), or 'acquiesce'.
If using *condone* in this sense note that it implies a certain amount of
shared guilt in failing to punish or prevent something: *Nixon may not
have planned the Watergate break-in, but he certainly condoned it.*

conduit The most common British pronunciation is with the stress on
the first syllable [**con**-jewit]. The US pronunciation is [**carn**-do-it].

confident An adjective meaning trusting or bold. Note the ending
-*ent*. A *confidant* (male) or *confidante* (female) is someone that you
confide in.

conjunction This is a grammatical part of speech that serves to
connect words, phrases, and clauses. Coordinating conjunctions link
parts of equal grammatical value; *and, but*, and *or* are the most common.
Subordinating conjunctions link subordinate clauses to the main clause
in a sentence; among the most common are *if*, *when*, and *though*.

In the sentence *He ran but he could not hide*, the coordinating
conjunction *but* links the two main clauses. In the sentence *He hid when
he could*, the subordinating conjunction *when* links the subordinate
clause to the main clause, *He hid*. Other common subordinating
conjunctions are *because, unless, after, than*, and *where*.

conjuror *or* **conjurer** This word may be spelled either way.

connection *or* **connexion** This word can be spelled either way.

connoisseur The standard British pronunciation is with the stress on
the first syllable and a weak second syllable [**con**-uh-sir]. The American
pronunciation also has the stress on the first syllable, and the final *r* is
pronounced.

conscientious Spelling: remember the **sc**.

consensus Spelling: remember the three **ss**.

consist, comprise, constitute, *or* **compose** To **consist** of
something is to be made up of it: *The programme consisted of two short
plays*. To **comprise** something has the same meaning, often implying
that the whole is regarded from the point of view of its individual parts:
The programme comprises two short plays (they were chosen to make it
up). To **constitute** something is to form a whole, especially of dissimilar
components: *Wealth and health do not necessarily constitute happiness*.
To **compose** means the same, but implies that the components have
something in common: *Water is composed of hydrogen and oxygen*. A

common mistake is to confuse *consist* and *comprise*, saying, for example:*The programme is comprised of two short plays*.

console See ◊condole.

consonant Any of the twenty-one letters of the English alphabet that are not vowels.

constitute See ◊consist.

consummate This word may be pronounced differently depending on whether it is an adjective, as in *a consummate victory*, or a verb, as in *to consummate a marriage*. Whereas the verb may be pronounced with the stress on the first syllable and has a weak second syllable [**con**-ser-mate], the adjective is pronounced with the stress on the second syllable [k'n-**sum**-mit] .

contagious See ◊infectious.

contemporary This is often used to mean 'modern', especially when referring to style or design. Its main meaning is 'belonging to the same time'. Strictly speaking a Victorian house with *contemporary* furniture would be furnished in Victorian, not modern, style.

contemptible *or* **contemptuous** A person or thing is **contemptible** if they are despised or held in contempt for some reason: *Stealing that money was a contemptible thing to do*. **Contemptuous** means that the person expresses contempt for someone or something else: *When I said I was sorry he simply gave me a contemptuous look*.

continual, continuous, *or* **constant** Something is **continual** if it happens repeatedly: *Our holiday was ruined by the continual rain* (it rained often but not all the time). It is **continuous** if it goes on without a break: *Our holiday was ruined by the continuous rain* (it rained all the time). If something is **constant** it happens many times in the same manner: *Ruth suffered from constant colds as a child*.

contrary *or* **converse** If a thing is **contrary** it either differs or disagrees: *I took the contrary view, that we should go by train rather than drive*. If something is **converse** it is the opposite: *I held the converse view: that museums should be privatized, not nationalized*.

In the sense 'differing' *contrary* is pronounced with the stress on the first syllable. In its other sense, 'perverse', it is pronounced with the stress on the second syllable, so that the end rhymes with *Mary*.

contribute The standard British pronunciation is with the stress on the second syllable [con-**trib**-yoot]. The pronunciation with the stress on the first syllable [**con**-trib-yoot] is increasingly heard, but is widely disapproved of. The US pronunciation has the stress on the second syllable.

controversial Spelling: note the **o** in the middle, not an **a**.

controversy The most educated British speakers prefer the pronunciation with the stress on the first syllable. The pronunciation with the stress on the second syllable is widely used, but disapproved of by some people. The US pronunciation has the stress on the first syllable.

converse See ◊contrary.

convince *and* **persuade** These can often be used interchangeably: *I persuaded* (or convinced) *him that we needed a new car*; *He was convinced* (or persuaded) *of the need for a new car*. However, **convince** means specifically 'to persuade someone to believe something', so it should not be used with a verb referring to an action: *I convinced him that he should buy a new car* (I made him believe that he should), but: *I persuaded him to buy a new car*.

cord *or* **chord** A **cord** is strong string or something resembling it: *I'll tie the door back with this cord*; *The choirmaster was testing the soloist's vocal cords*. A **chord** has various specialized senses, such as a straight line in mathematics or a simultaneous sounding of musical notes. (It can also be used of vocal chords.) Figuratively, it has the musical sense when referring to an emotional response: *The mother's TV appeal struck a deep chord with many viewers*.

co-respondent See ◊correspondent.

corporal *or* **corporeal** Corporal is to do directly with the body: *Corporal punishment is now mostly a thing of the past*. **Corporeal** is used of something that is intended for the body or that has a bodily substance: *Hospitals not only treat patients but attend to their corporeal needs* (i.e. provide them with food and drink); *Ghosts do not have a corporeal existence*.

correlate Spelling: remember that the beginning is **cor-** (Latin 'with'), not **co-**.

correspondent *or* **co-respondent** A **correspondent** is a person one writes to regularly: *My pen friend and I have been correspondents since we were teenagers*. A **co-respondent** is (or was) a person (usually a man) accused of committing adultery in a divorce case, the other person (usually a woman) being the respondent: *He was cited as co-respondent*.

coruscating (meaning 'sparkling'). Spelling: note the single **r**.

cosiness Spelling: the **y** in *cosy* changes to an **i**.

cosy US spelling: *cozy*.

council *or* **counsel** A **council** is a body of people who meet for discussion or consultation: *The parish council meets once a month.* **Counsel** is advice: *'Take my counsel, happy man;/Act upon it, if you can!'* (W S Gilbert). The two senses are reflected in **councillor** for a member of a council and **counsellor** for an official adviser. Try to remember this distinction when spelling the two words. However, members of the Privy Council, the sovereign's advisory committee, can be Privy Counsellors (the historic spelling) or Privy Councillors.

counsel See ▷council.

counterfeit Spelling: note the **ei**.

courteous, courtesy Both these words are stressed on the first syllable, which is pronounced [curt].

cousin The word **cousin** is used loosely to refer to any relative of the same generation, other than brothers and sisters. Your *first cousins* are the children of your parents' brothers and sisters. Your *second cousins* are the children of your parents' first cousins; their children will be *third cousins* to your children.

The term *removed* can be used when referring to the children or parents of cousins. Your first cousins' children are your *first cousins once removed*, their children will be your *first cousins twice removed*. Your second cousins' parents are your *second cousins once removed*, their parents are *twice removed*, and so on.

It is seldom necessary to specify the exact relationship; in everyday use any cousin's children are called simply *nieces* and *nephews* and their parents *uncles* and *aunts*. The term *cousin-in-law*, to refer to your partner's cousins or your cousins' partners, exists but is seldom used. It is just as easy, and more specific, to say *my husband's cousin* or *my cousin's wife*.

covert The traditional pronunciation is like *covered* except that it ends with a **t** sound, but an alternative pronunciation [**koh**-vert], in which the second syllable rhymes with *Bert* is increasingly heard, especially in contexts of espionage and other clandestine activities.

crape *or* **crêpe** Crape is a black silk or cotton material with a wrinkled surface: *Mourners formerly wore crape armbands.* **Crêpe** is a light thin material with a wrinkled surface: *Margaret looked elegant in her white crêpe de Chine blouse.*

credence *or* **credit** To give **credence** to something is to believe it: *I find it hard to give credence to his explanation* (I don't believe it). To give **credit** to something is to believe in it: *I don't give any credit to that theory* (I don't trust it); *Would you credit it!* (Would you believe such a thing).

credible, creditable, *or* **credulous** **Credible** is used of something that can be believed: *It seems hardly credible that last weekend we were still abroad.* **Creditable** is used of something that deserves praise or credit: *The gymnast gave a highly creditable performance.* **Credulous** is used of a person who is gullible or all too readily believes things: *He was a credulous child, and thought the stories they told him were true.* People sometimes use **credible** when they mean *credulous.*

credit See ▷credence.

creditable See ▷credible.

credulous See ▷credible.

crêpe See ▷crape.

crescendo *Crescendo* is a term in music meaning a passage which gradually increases in volume (it comes from an Italian word meaning 'to increase or grow'). *Crescendo* can also be used for any gradual increase in force or effect, leading up to a climax: *a crescendo of excitement which culminated when the Queen appeared on the balcony.* It is often used as though it meant the climax itself, in phrases such as *rise to a crescendo; reach a crescendo*, although many people consider this to be incorrect.

crevice *or* **crevasse** A **crevice** is a narrow opening in something such as a wall or a rock: *The birds had built their nests in the crevices of the cliff.* A **crevasse** is a deep open crack in the ice of a glacier: *The polar explorers had to negotiate several dangerous crevasses.*

culminate This means 'to reach the highest or final point', and is usually used figuratively. It implies a gradual development, not a sudden act: *A history of bad luck and bad management which culminated in bankruptcy.*

curb *or* **kerb** Use **curb** to mean 'restrain' or 'restraint', and **kerb** to mean the edge of the pavement. In American English, however, *curb* is used for all meanings.

currant This word, meaning a small fruit, and ending **-ant**, should not be confused with *current* which has several meanings including 'running', 'flowing', and 'present'.

curriculum Spelling: note the double **r**.

curriculum vitae This Latin expression is the full formal term for a written summary of a person's education, qualifications, skills, and job history. The word *vitae* is pronounced [**vee**-tie]. The abbreviation *cv* is usually used in conversation, and is also very common in writing. Americans are more likely to use *biodata* or *résumé*, and make less use of the form in any case. You may be asked to supply a cv when you apply for a job, or if you apply for a place on a course.

Do not aim to produce an all-purpose cv. Rather aim to produce one suitable for the present application. Select the information that is relevant to the requirements of the particular job. If you are given a job description, use it to help you select and give weight to certain pieces of information. Your aim is to show what makes you eligible for this particular job. Unless you are sure that your place in the county hockey team is relevant, leave it out.

You will need to organize the information you provide in your cv. Put your name and the title *curriculum vitae* or *cv* at the beginning with the date. A typical cv might be organized into seven or eight sections. Start with a section headed *Personal Details*. Give your address, telephone number, nationality, if relevant, and date of birth.

The thing which is most important to a possible employer is your most recent work and responsibilities, so the second section might be headed *Present Work*. Next in importance may be your qualifications, so in the third section you could list them. If you are at the beginning of your working life, you may want to mention the secondary school(s) you attended.

A prospective employer will want to have an outline of your job history. Organize this by giving for each job firstly the starting and finishing dates. Give the title of the post. If you had experiences, responsibilities, or special training that would help you to do the job that you are applying for, describe them. Account for the whole of your working life. Do not leave gaps that may make the employer wonder if you are reliable.

Employers usually ask for referees, and specify how many and who they should be. The last section of your cv should give details of them. They will be people who can bear witness to your abilities in fields relevant to the job you are applying for. They should be able to say how your personal qualities make you suitable. One will usually be your present employer. As well as names, give the positions in their organizations of your referees, and their current addresses.

Other things that you might mention in a cv, if relevant, are the languages you speak, the fact that you hold a driving licence, any part you have played in the social organization of your workplaces, and your outside interests.

cynical *or* **sceptical** A **cynical** person is one who sneers or mocks, especially about someone or something normally held in high esteem: *Whenever my father visits the doctor he makes some cynical remark about 'seeing the quack'.* A **sceptical** person is dubious or mistrustful: *She seemed sceptical when I said we'd be back by teatime.*

cypher *or* **cipher** This word can be spelled either way.

czar, tsar, *or* **tzar** This word can be spelled in all three ways.

dais This word has two syllables, and is pronounced [**day**-iss]. Spelling: note the **ai**.

dangling participle *or* **hanging participle** *or* **unattached participle** *Walking back home yesterday, a tree nearly fell on my head.* If strict logic is applied to that sentence, it should mean that the tree was walking back home: the subject of the main clause of a sentence (here, *a tree*) is assumed to be the subject of a phrase attached to the main clause – as in *Being shy, she never said a word.*

But language does not always keep to the tramlines of strict logic, and it is quite common to find attached phrases applying to some other part of the main clause (here, the 'I' implied by *my head*). Such phrases usually contain participles: they are called dangling participles, or hanging participles, or unattached participles. In the sentence above, the dangling participle is a present participle *walking*, but you can also have a dangling past participle: *If properly secured, you shouldn't be able to remove the cover.*

Dangling participles are not considered acceptable in standard English, so they should be avoided in writing. Recast offending sentences so that the subject of the attached phrase is clear: *As I was walking back home yesterday a tree nearly fell on my head; If the cover is properly secured, you shouldn't be able to remove it.*

dash This is a punctuation mark (–) that can be used singly or in pairs (as a type of parenthesis, to mark off a clearly subordinate part of a sentence). A single dash is used to represent a sudden break or interruption in dialogue or an abrupt change of subject.

A sentence should not have more than one pair of dashes. For marking off a clause or phrase integral to the structure of the sentence, commas are preferred: *Then Alan, who is always hungry, decided it was time for lunch.*

In dialogue, dashes represent a sudden break or interruption, whereas hesitation is usually indicated by ellipsis (three dots). *I think I know – now, don't tell me. It's next to ... to – no, that's the other – I give up.*

A dash can also give a special emphasis to the end of a sentence. *Seeing the door slightly ajar, he gave it a push and it opened to reveal Agnes – in the arms of Fred!*

data Strictly speaking, *data* is the plural of *datum*, and means 'a fact', 'a piece of information'. It is often used as another word for information, followed by a singular verb: *Data is stored on the computer*. This is now regarded as acceptable, especially in American English and in the language of information technology.

By far the most general pronunciation is [**day**-ter], though a few people prefer the traditional Latin pronunciation [**dar**-ter].

dates To express a date as day-month-year, the preferred British style in formal writing is: *On 10 July 1994 the parliament sat for the first time*. The other British style, also used in the USA, is: *On July 10, 1994, the parliament sat for the first time*.

In informal notes, official forms, invoices etc, people sometimes use an all-figure form of the date, for example, 12.9.94. Do not use this form in international contexts, because British and American practice is different. In Britain the date is read as day-month-year, whereas in the USA it is read as month-day-year. So, while in Britain 2.9.94. would be read as the second of September 1994, in the USA it would be read as the ninth of February 1994. If you meet an all-figure form of the date in an international context, be aware that it is likely to need the American interpretation.

Material produced on a computer often has an all-figure form of the date. Note that in this the numbers 1 to 9 are preceded by zero, and only the last two digits of the year are used. In Britain the second of September 1994 would have the form 02 09 94. However, many computer programs are designed in the USA, and some automatically put the day's date on a document. In this case it will be the American form, with month before day, unless you change it.

If the year is not given, the preferred style is to spell out the day of the month: *the session of the tenth of July*. The alternative is: *the session of 10 July*. When only month and year are given, the preferred style is without punctuation: *July 1994*

When **centuries** are mentioned, spell them out without using capital letters: *the fourteenth century*; *the mid-twentieth century*; *nineteenth-century reforms*. In cases such as the last example, where the century comes before a noun, hyphens are used by some British writers, but the current trend is towards the American practice of leaving them out.

There are two ways of referring to a **decade**. In an essay or report use the number of the year plus **s**: *in the 1940s*. It is no longer usual to put an apostrophe before the **s**. In informal writing and newspaper features the abbreviated form of the word is often used: *in the forties*.

The abbreviations AD and BC stand for *Anno Domini*, which is Latin for 'the Year of Our Lord', and *Before Christ*. These abbreviations may be written with or without full stops. AD always goes before the number of the year, and BC goes after it. *Tiberius lived from 42 BC to AD 37*.

For information on dates in letters, see ◊letter writing. For information on quoting the dates of publications, see ◊essay and report writing.

deadly *or* **deathly** If something is **deadly** it is either literally fatal or, less commonly, suggests death: *The insect is well known for its deadly sting*; *She was deadly pale*. If something is **deathly** it may be literally fatal but is more likely to suggest a dead state: *His face was deathly pale*.

debar *or* **disbar** To **debar** someone is to bar or exclude them from a place or prevent them from exercising a right: *Women are debarred from some London clubs*; *People under 18 are debarred from voting*. To **disbar** someone means the same, but the word is used mainly in a legal context: *The barrister was disbarred* (expelled from the Bar).

debtor Spelling: note the **b** as in *debt*, and the ending **-or**.

decade The standard way of saying it is [**deck**- aid] with the stress on the first syllable. A pronunciation the same as that of *decayed* is widely used but disapproved of.

decimate This comes from the Latin *decimare*, meaning 'take the tenth man', and means 'kill or remove one in ten of'. It is now often used to mean 'damage severely', 'destroy or kill most of': *Tuberculosis decimated the population*; *Cheap imports decimated the coal industry*. Many people deplore this, both because of the meaning and because of the use of decimate with a single entity: you cannot destroy one in ten of the coal industry, although you may close one pit in ten. However, this usage is now very common, and seems likely to become accepted.

decrepit Spelling: note the **t** on the end, not a **d**.

defence US spelling: *defense*.

definite *or* **definitive** If something is **definite** it is certain or clear: *There was a definite chill in the air*; *I'll give you a definite answer tomorrow* (a straight one). If a thing is **definitive** it is final and authoritative: *This is the definitive version of the story; I'll give you a definitive answer tomorrow* (one that will settle it).

definite article See ▷article.

definitely It is easy to misspell this word. Remember the two **is** in the middle.

definitive See ▷definite.

deity Both [**day**-uh-tee] and [**dee**-uh-tee] are common and accepted pronunciations.

delicatessen Spelling: note the single **l** and **t**.

delineate Spelling: note the single **l** and the **e** after the **n**.

delusion *or* **illusion** A **delusion** is a strong belief that a thing is really other than it is: *The patient was under the delusion that the potatoes they gave him were rocks* (they were obviously not). An **illusion** is a deception caused by a thing appearing to be other than it really is as in a magician's trick.

demonstrable The most common British pronunciation begins like the word *delight* and is stressed on the second syllable [di-**mon**-strable]. The pronunciation with the stress on the first syllable [**dem**-n-strable] is preferred by purists. Americans only use the form stressed on the second syllable.

demur Spelling: note the ending **-ur**, not **-er**.

denouement Spelling: remember the **e** after the **ou**.

dependent *or* **dependant** Dependent is the adjective, used for a person or thing that depends on someone or something: *Admission to college is dependent on A-level results.* **Dependant** is the noun, and is a person who relies on someone for financial support: *Do you have any dependants?* In American English, the noun can also be spelled *dependent*.

depraved *or* **deprived** Someone who is **depraved** is morally bad or corrupt: *He was utterly depraved, and had a bad influence on many of his colleagues.* Someone who is **deprived** lacks the normal benefits of food, clothing, housing, and the like: *The council was particularly concerned about the number of deprived children on the estate.*

deprecate *or* **depreciate** Deprecate means to deplore something, **depreciate** means to belittle something or to treat it as unimportant.

However, *self-deprecating*, in the sense 'disparaging oneself', 'modestly understating one's own abilities' has become firmly established, although some people deprecate this usage.

depredation Spelling: remember the **e** after the **r**.

deprived See ▷depraved.

derisive *or* **derisory** Derisive is used of something that conveys contempt: *The driver answered the traffic warden with a derisive gesture.* **Derisory** is used of something that invites contempt or scorn: *The workers were offered a derisory pay increase.*

derogate See ▷abdicate.

descendant Spelling: remember the **-ant** at the end.

desert *or* **dessert** When stressed on the second syllable, **desert** means something that is deserved, especially in the plural: *He got his just deserts*; *'According to their deserts will I judge them'* (Bible: Ezekiel 7.27). **Dessert** is the sweet course of a meal: *We had a straightforward lunch: starter, main course, and dessert.*

desiccated Spelling: think of **de** plus **siccated** so that you remember it has one **s** and two **c**s.

designer This has been used since the 1960s to refer to items, particularly fashionable clothing, bearing the name of a famous designer, with the implication that they were superior and expensive: *Designer jeans from leading fashion houses.* It has become a cliché, and is now mainly used humorously, with the implication that the 'designer' item is overrated or merely trendy.

despatch See ▷dispatch.

desperate Spelling: remember the **e** in the middle.

despicable The first syllable is the same as the first syllable of *despise*, and the word is pronounced [di-**spick**-able]. Some traditionalists still use the older pronunciation [**dess**-pick-able], with the stress on the first syllable, but it is rarely heard.

dessert See ▷desert.

detach Spelling: remember it has no **t** before the **ch**.

determiner A word like *the, a, some* or *this*, which is placed before a noun and defines the particular noun you are talking about.

developing Spelling: remember it has only one **l** and one **p**.

dexterous *or* **dextrous** This word can be spelled either way.

diagram Spelling: remember it is not **-mme** at the end.

diarrhoea US spelling: *diarrhea*.

dichotomy The first syllable is pronounced [die]. The stress is on the second syllable [**cot**]. Spelling: note the **ch**.

dietician *or* **dietitian** This word can be spelled either way.

different The verb *to differ* can be followed only by *from*, and some people apply the same rule to *different*. However, different *to* has been in use since the 15th century, and is quite acceptable. Different *than*, once quite common, is no longer considered correct in British English, but is the standard form in American English.

dike See ◊dyke.

dilapidated Spelling: note that it has a single **l** and single **p**.

dilatory The stress is on the first syllable, the second syllable is weak, and the *o* is lost altogether [**dill**-uh-tree].

dilemma This means a choice, or a situation demanding a choice, between equally undesirable alternatives; a doctor at a difficult birth would be *in a dilemma* if he could save the mother or the child, but not both. Some people maintain that it should not be used when there are more than two alternatives, and it is best to avoid referring to a complex problem, with many possible courses of action, as a dilemma: *the dilemma of economic decline*. A dilemma may have more than two choices, but they should be few in number and clearly defined: *the dilemma of whether to go on to short-time working, lay off staff, or cut wages*. Strictly speaking, *dilemma* should not be used if the choices are pleasant or unimportant; having to choose between cream and ice cream on your strawberries is hardly a dilemma.

dilettante The stress is on the third syllable [**tan**]. The word comes from Italian, and the final **e** is pronounced, giving [diller-**tan**-tee]. Spelling: note the single **l** and double **t**.

dinghy (a type of boat). Spelling: remember the **h**.

dingy (meaning dirty). Spelling: Remember that there is no **e**.

diphtheria Spelling: remember the **ph**.

diphthong Spelling: remember the **ph**.

disappear Spelling: think of **dis** plus **appear**, and remember one **s** and two **ps**.

disappoint Spelling: think of **dis** plus **appoint**, and remember one **s** and two **ps**.

disapprove Spelling: think of **dis** plus **approve**, and remember one **s** and two **ps**.

disbar See ⟩debar.

disc *or* **disk** In British English **disc** is the usual spelling, but American English uses *disk*, and **disk** is also more common in computing, as in *disk drive*.

discomfort *or* **discomfiture** Discomfort is pain, unease or embarrassment: *Linda's sprained wrist caused her continuing discomfort*; *I had to face the discomfort of telling them myself*. To experience **discomfiture** is to feel disconcerted, or baffled: *He laughed at my momentary discomfiture at the arrival of the unexpected guest*.

discreet *or* **discrete** Discreet relates to modesty or reserve, otherwise discretion: *We must be discreet about this in case he suspects something*. **Discrete** is used of things that have been separated into distinct parts: *The coroner's task was to reconcile the discrete events that led to the death*.

disingenuous See ⟩ingenious.

disinterested *or* **uninterested** If you are **disinterested** in something you are impartial and do not take sides: *A disinterested observer of the scene would have wondered what all the fuss was about*. If you are **uninterested** you have no interest at all: *The player was uninterested in the public reaction to his remark*. *Disinterested* is often used instead of *uninterested* to mean lacking interest. This use is widely regarded as incorrect and should be avoided, especially in formal writing.

disk See ⟩disc.

dismissal Spelling: remember the single **s** and then double **s**.

dispatch *or* **despatch** This word can be spelled either way, although *dispatch* is more common.

dispirited Spelling: remember there is only one **s**.

dispute The verb and noun are both pronounced with the stress on the second syllable [diss-**pyoot**]. A sizeable number of speakers pronounce the noun with the stress on the first syllable [**diss**-pyoot]. Both pronunciations are acceptable.

dissatisfied Spelling: remember the double **s**.

dissect *or* **bisect** To **dissect** something is to cut it into pieces or analyze it: *The pathologist dissected the body*; *The new film was dissected by the critics*. (The word begins with *dis-*, 'apart', not *di-*, 'two'). To **bisect** something is to cut it into two: *The path bisected the park*.

disseminate Spelling: remember the double **s**. It comes from the Latin *dis* meaning 'asunder' and *seminare*, 'to sow'.

dissension Spelling: note the double **s** and the ending **-sion**, not **-tion**.

dissent *or* **dissension** Dissent is the opposite of assent, so refers to a difference of opinion: *Some Russian dissidents were not afraid to voice their dissent from Communist party policy*. **Dissension** is angry or heated disagreement: *The management's proposal was the cause of much dissension among the workforce.*◊See also dissenting.

dissenting, dissident, *or* **dissentient** Dissenting means disagreeing: *There was only one dissenting vote when we took a show of hands*. **Dissident** means the same, but implies a stronger or more personally felt disagreement, especially with the authorities: *There were many dissident writers in Soviet Russia keen to make their opinions felt*. **Dissentient** also means the same, but emphasizes the difference between those who disagree and the majority: *The Liberal Democrats became the dissentient voices of British politics in the 1980s and were critical of both the main parties*.

dissertation Spelling: remember the double **s**.

dissident See ◊dissenting.

dissipate Spelling: note the double **s** and single **p**.

dissociate Spelling: remember it is not *dis-* **as**-*sociate*.

distil Spelling: note the single **l**, although American English uses *distill*.

distinct *or* **distinctive** Distinct is used of something clearly apparent or obvious: *There has been a distinct improvement in the weather this month*. **Distinctive** is used of something that can be distinguished in some way or that stands out by being different: *The singer had a distinctive voice that won her many fans.*

distracted See ⟩distraught.

distraught, distracted, *or* **distrait** A **distraught** person usually behaves irrationally when affected by a deep emotion such as fear or grief: *The distraught mother looked for the missing child everywhere.* A **distracted** person is often one who is mentally confused or even insane, even if only temporarily: *The poor woman was quite distracted and kept murmuring the same words over and over again.* A person who is **distrait** is absent-minded (ie abstracted rather than distracted): *My fellow guest appeared gloomy and distrait, and I wondered what was troubling him.*

distribute The standard British pronunciation is with the stress on the second syllable [dis-**trib**-yoot]. The pronunciation with the stress on the first syllable [**dis**-trib-yoot] is increasingly heard, but is widely disapproved of. The US pronunciation has the stress on the second syllable.

distrust *or* **mistrust** **Distrust** implies an absence of trust: *He has an innate distrust of foreigners.* **Mistrust**, the weaker word, implies a hesitation to trust: *He lacked confidence, and mistrusted his own judgment in such things.*

diverse *or* **divers** **Diverse** is used of things that are different or varied: *There were diverse opinions about the matter.* **Divers**, an old-fashioned or literary word, means that there are simply various things or a number of them: *And he healed many that were sick of divers diseases* (Bible: Mark 1.34).

Domesday *or* **doomsday** **Domesday** is the usual spelling for the Domesday Book, while **Doomsday** is Judgement Day and **doomsday** is this same word in a general sense: *The Domesday Book was probably so called as there was no appeal against it, any more than there was against Doomsday; This work will take me till doomsday.*

double negative *She didn't see nothing.* Did she see anything? In many varieties of English, the answer would be a clear 'no'. It is common to reinforce the negativeness of a sentence by using two (or even more) negative words. So *She didn't see nothing* is the same as *She certainly didn't see anything.*

From a mathematical point of view, however, two negatives equal a positive, and it has come to be thought that sentences like *She didn't see nothing* should mean 'She did see something'. In practice, no one would ever interpret them like that unless the context suggested it, but such *double negatives* are not regarded as acceptable in standard English. Say instead, *She didn't see anything* or *She saw nothing*.

It is particularly easy to fall into the double negative trap after expressions like *I shouldn't be surprised if* and *I shouldn't wonder if*. There is a great temptation to put in another negative word, even though what you want to say is positive: *I shouldn't be surprised if it didn't rain.* If what you mean is that you expect it to rain, say *I shouldn't be surprised if it rained.*

There is one sort of double negative that is accepted in standard English. You can use *not* with a word that has a negative prefix, in order to emphasize positive meaning – as in *a not inconsiderable sum* and *a not unreasonable question*. The technical name for this is litotes, pronounced [lie-**tote**-ees].

doubling letters See ◊spelling rules.

doubtful *or* **dubious** If something is **doubtful** it is uncertain, and one needs to know more about it: *The weather looks doubtful* (it may rain, but it may not). If a thing is **dubious** it raises or causes doubt: *He gave a dubious reply when I asked him about it*; *Christine had the rather dubious privilege of staying behind to keep an eye on things*.

douse *or* **dowse** To **douse** something is to extinguish it: *We doused the blaze with buckets of water*; *Hey, douse that light!* To **dowse** is to search for water underground by using a special divining rod: *A dowsing party soon established the presence of an underground stream*. However, *douse* can also be spelled *dowse* in the first sense.

draft *or* **draught** A **draft** is either a preliminary written version of something or a body of people selected for a special purpose: *The solicitor had prepared a draft of the letter he intended to send*; *A second draft of troops was called in to assist in the flooded area*. A **draught** is a current of air or a swallowing of liquid: *There's a terrible draught in here*; *He downed his glass of beer in a single draught*. In American English the usual spelling is *draft* for both senses.

dual *or* **duel** **Dual** is an adjective relating to anything that there are two of: *A public path and a stretch of grass separated the house from the dual carriageway*. **Duel** is a noun, and is the formal fight or contest between two people: *The men arranged to meet in a duel at dawn*.

dubious See ◊doubtful.

due to Although it is very common, many people object to *due to* being used to introduce the reason for an undesirable situation, maintaining that *owing to* is the correct form: *Due* (or owing) *to the fog, all flights were delayed for several hours*. There is no real reason to avoid *due to*, but it is just as easy to use *because of*, which no one can criticize.

duel See ⏵dual.

duffel *or* **duffle** This word can be spelled either way.

dyke This is the usual British spelling, although American English uses *dike*.

dynasty In Britain the standard pronunciation is [**din**-er-stee], in the USA [**dine**-er-stee]. The broadcasting in Britain of the American soap opera *Dynasty* in the 1980s familiarized British speakers with the transatlantic pronunciation.

dysentery Spelling: remember the **y** at the beginning and the ending **-ery**.

each In traditional standard English, the pronoun **each** is used with a singular verb and singular pronouns: *Each has made his own decision*.

As with other indefinite pronouns, which could refer to either a man or a woman, there is a tendency in present-day English to use a plural verb and pronouns with it (see ▷they/their/theirs). But the conjunction of *each* and *have* in *Each have made their own decision* is inelegant, and the use of a singular verb and a plural pronoun in *Each has made their own decision* is scarcely better, so it is preferable to avoid this construction altogether by using an *of* phrase: *Each of them have made their own decision*.

When **each** comes after a plural noun or pronoun, it takes a plural verb: *They each have their own way of doing it*.

easiness Spelling: remember the **i** in the middle, not a **y**.

eatable *or* **edible** Eatable is used of something that is in a fit state to be eaten: *The school lunches were sometimes barely eatable*. **Edible** can also be used in this way, but is frequently reserved for something that can basically be eaten or serve as food: *Are these berries edible?*

ebullient The standard pronunciation is with the stress on the second syllable, which is pronounced like the **bul-** in *bulb*. The pronunciation is [ee- **bul**ee-uhnt].

eclectic See ▷esoteric.

economic *or* **economical** Economic pertains to economy (or to the economy), or to something that is profitable: *Business leaders looked eagerly for signs of an economic recovery*; *It's not really economic to run buses on all the routes*. **Economical** relates to a person or thing that economizes, or is not wasteful: *She is economical by nature and keeps a regular note of her expenses*.

ecstasy Spelling: remember **cs**, not **x**, and the ending **-asy**.

eczema Spelling: remember **cz**, not **x**.

edible See ▷eatable.

effect See ▷affect and ▷impact.

effective, effectual, efficacious, *or* **efficient** If something is **effective** it has a noticeable effect: *The actor made a most effective entrance.* If it is **effectual** it produces a particular effect, usually the one intended: *We took effectual steps to redress the situation.* If a thing is **efficacious** it has the power or potential to produce a particular effect: *These tablets are efficacious against malaria.* If a thing is **efficient** it works well: *Josie did a very efficient job with the lawns.*

effeminate *or* **effete** Effeminate, as used of a man, means 'not manly', in other words 'womanish': *Adam has a slightly effeminate way of walking.* **Effete** is now also used in this sense, but more exactly means feeble or even decadent because over- refined: *The uniform of long blue coat, yellow stockings and black buckled shoes gave the boys a rather effete appearance.*

efficacious See ▷effective.

efficient See ▷effective.

e.g. *or* **i.e.** The abbreviation **e.g.** (from the Latin *exempli gratia*, 'for sake of an example') indicates that one or more examples follow of what has been mentioned in general terms: *It could be cheaper by public transport, e.g. by train or coach.* The abbreviation **i.e.** (from the Latin *id est*, 'that is') indicates that an explanation follows of what has just been mentioned: *Gratuities are discretionary, i.e. you don't have to leave a tip if you don't want to.*

egoist *or* **egotist** There is a considerable overlap between the words, but a difference exists. An **egoist** is someone who is self-centred or selfish, often without realising it: *He's a proper egoist, never thinking to enquire about the needs or wishes of anyone else.* An **egotist** is an arrogant or conceited person, always talking about himself: *She's a real egotist, always on about what she has done or is planning to do.*

egregious The pronunciation is with the stress on the second syllable. The first syllable is like the beginning of *elope*, and the word is pronounced [i-**gree**-jus].

either Either on its own is used with a singular verb: *Wear red or white – either is acceptable.* When it is followed by *of*, it commonly has a plural verb: *Have either of you seen my glasses?*, although in formal writing a singular verb is preferable: *Has either of you seen my glasses?*.

When it is followed by *or*, the verb agrees with the noun or pronoun that comes after the *or*. If this is singular, the verb is singular: *Either John or Kathie has got it*. But if it is plural, the verb is plural: *Either Frankie or his brothers have promised to be there*.

The second noun or pronoun also determines the person of the verb: *Either you or I am right*, but *Either I or you are right*.

If one noun or pronoun refers to a male person and the other to a female person, it is permissible to use a plural verb and plural pronouns, in order to avoid the invidious 'he': *If either Peter or Jennie ring, tell them I'll call them back*.

When you use **either ... or**, it is preferable to put both the *either* and the *or* immediately in front of the parts of the sentence they refer to. So: *You must either pay up or leave* is more acceptable than: *Either you must pay up or leave*, and: *You can have either red wine or white* is more acceptable than: *You can either have red wine or white*.

When **either** is a pronoun, it refers only to two things or people: *Has either of you two seen Harry?* For three or more things or people, use *any*. But when *either* is a conjunction, it is perfectly acceptable to use it for three or more things or people: *For the first course, you can have either soup, pâté or fruit juice*.

As an adjective, **either** can mean either 'one or the other of two': *She can write with either hand* or 'each': *There's a lifeguard station at either end of the beach*. But be aware that when you use it in a context which could have both meanings, you may cause confusion: if you say, *There's a service tunnel that runs on either side of the main tunnel*, do you mean that there is one service tunnel that runs first on the left side of the main tunnel, then on the right, then on the left, and so on, or that there are two service tunnels, one on each side of the main tunnel?

The main British pronunciation of **either** is with[**aye**]. There is an alternative with [**ee**], but this is frowned upon by some. The main US pronunciation is [**ee**-the], but [**aye**-the] is also heard. See also ◊neither.

elder *or* **older** Elder is used in family or professional relationships: *His elder brother is called John*; *I was the elder partner in the business*. **Older** is used in a general sense: *She's not much older than me*. Both have the same meaning, but while *older* can refer to people or things, *elder* is applied only to people. Your *elder* sister can be any sister older than you, including your *eldest* sister, the first-born. *Elder* should not be used after the noun: *My elder* (or older) *sister is two years older than me*.

embarrass Spelling: remember the double **r** and double **s**.

embodiment Spelling: remember the **i**, not a **y**.

emend See ◊amend.

emotional *or* **emotive** **Emotional** is used of something that expresses emotion or that is affected by emotion: *He read us an emotional account of his loss*; *There's no need to be so emotional: crying like that won't help matters*. **Emotive** is used of something that has the potential to affect the emotions, but that may not necessarily do so: *Abortion tends to be a very emotive subject*.

empathy See ◊sympathy.

enervate *or* **invigorate** Because of a false association with words such as elevate and energy, **enervate** is often used to mean 'invigorate'. It actually means the opposite: to drain and weaken: *The climate in hot countries can be depressing and enervating*. To **invigorate** someone or something thus means to give them vigour and energy: *The freshness of the morning invigorated me as I walked*.

enforceable Spelling: remember to keep the **e** before adding **able**.

England *and* **English** These are often used carelessly as though they applied to the whole of the United Kingdom. This makes many Scots, Welsh, and Irish people angry. See ◊Britain.

enormousness *or* **enormity** **Enormousness** relates to the state of being much larger than expected: *She was stunned by the enormousness of the task of feeding everyone*. **Enormity** properly refers to something that is outrageously or horrifyingly large, such as a crime: *James was appalled at the enormity of the theft*. *Enormity* is often used to mean 'enormousness' but many people regard this as incorrect.

enquire *or* **inquire** This word can be spelled either way, although the tendency is to use **enquire** when asking for information, and **inquire** when conducting an investigation.

ensure See ◊assure.

enthuse **Enthuse**, meaning 'to be *or* to make someone enthusiastic', 'to show enthusiasm', originated in the USA and is still regarded as an Americanism by many people. Avoid using it in formal speech or writing.

envelope The majority of British speakers say [**enn**-ver-lope] but some, mainly older, speakers keep a pronunciation nearer to the French, and say [**on**-ver-lope].

envisage This is similar to *imagine*; it means to form a mental picture of something which may one day exist. It is often used to mean 'intend': *We do not envisage making changes in the near future*. This sounds pompous and also rather vague, implying that you have not really thought about the possibility of change. *We do not intend to make changes* is more definite, implying that you have made a conscious decision not to change.

epigram, epigraph, epitaph, *or* **epithet** An epigram, originally an inscription on a monument or statue, is now a short, witty statement, especially one with two counterbalancing halves: *Francis Bacon popularized the epigram: 'If the hill will not come to Mahomet, Mahomet will go to the hill'*. An **epigraph** is either an inscription on a monument or statue, or a motto or quotation at the beginning of a book: *The epigraph to E M Forster's novel* Howards End *is 'Only connect!'*.

An **epitaph** is an inscription on a tomb or grave: *Dryden's epitaph on his wife was: 'Here lies my wife: here let her lie!/Now she's at rest, and so am I'*. An **epithet** is an adjective or phrase describing a person or thing: *Richard Coeur de Lion earned the epithet 'Lionheart' because of his bravery*.

epigraph See ◊epigram.

epitaph See ◊epigram.

epithet See ◊epigram.

equable *or* **equitable** If a thing is **equable** it is unvarying in an agreeable way: *The island of Malta has an equable climate, with stable temperatures for most of the year*. If it is **equitable** it is impartial or reasonable: *The crew reached an equitable agreement: they would take it in turns to keep watch*.

equally *Equally* should not be followed by *as*: *He's equally as good as his brother*. Use *just as good*, or change the order of the sentence: *He and his brother are equally good*.

equitable The stress is on the first syllable. The British pronunciation is [**eck**-quitable]. American English has a weak second syllable [**eck**-kwuht-able]. See ◊equable.

erupt *or* **irrupt** To **erupt** is literally to burst out, while the less common **irrupt** is literally to burst in: *The gang erupted from the building onto the street when the police irrupted into it*.

Eskimo See ◊Indian.

esoteric *or* **eclectic** Something **esoteric** is designed for the select few or the initiated, with the implication that the thing in question is abstruse or obscure: *James Joyce's esoteric use of language can deter the average reader*. If a thing is **eclectic** (an *esoteric* word) it implies that the best of something has been selected from a number of sources, or simply that a person has wide or catholic tastes: *The concert was enjoyably eclectic, and included music from Bach to the Beatles*.

essay and report writing:

In this entry you will find advice about the conventions of presentation of essays and reports. For advice on expression and organization, see ◊plain English and ◊paragraph.

1. Organisation

An essay or report may consist solely of a title followed by the text. If any of the following are also included, they should come in this order before the text:

separate title page
summary
table of contents
list of illustrations
list of tables

At the end you may want appendices and a bibliography.

At the beginning you need, either at the top of the first sheet, or on a separate unnumbered sheet, the title or the question that you are answering, your name, and the date.

If a report is long, it may be useful to give a brief summary after the title so that those who do not have time to read the full report can know the gist, and those who are going to read it in full are in a better position to grasp what it is saying.

You will probably want to make the structure of a report or study apparent. One standard practice is to give each major section an Arabic numeral and a heading, and then to use letters and subheadings for the subsections. Try to avoid a third layer of organization, but if one is needed, use lower case Roman numerals, (i), (ii), (iii), etc.

An alternative is to use the decimal system, numbering major sections with Arabic numerals, and subsections with a major section numeral plus a point and a second numeral, e.g. 5.2. If a third layer is needed, use a second decimal place, e.g. 5.2.1.

If the text is long, you should have a contents page. On this you should list the major sections, by numbers and letters, if used, and headings. Under each heading give the numbers and letters of the subsections together with the subheadings, or give a brief indication of the topic covered in each. Use a new line for each section and subsection, and give page numbers for at least the major sections. The reader will find it helpful to be able to see the structure of the text at a glance.

2. References and quotes

In the course of the essay or report, you are likely to refer to sources such as books and articles. Possibly you will need to refer to magazines, works of art, poems, or songs. The conventions are these: Follow the use of capital letters in the original. Use italics for the titles of books, newspapers, magazines, plays, films, works of art, and long musical works. Use single quotation marks for articles, essays, stories, chapters, poems, television programmes, radio programmes, and songs. If you are handwriting or using a typewriter, you indicate italics by underlining.

When you quote from a book or article, you need to make clear which words are your own and which you are quoting. A short quotation should be placed in single inverted commas (double in the USA). A longer one can be presented as a block, i.e. separated from the text by a blank line top and bottom, and marked by wider margins. If anything is omitted from quoted material, put three ellipsis points – dots – in the space. If you, the writer, want to insert your own comment into a quotation, put it in square brackets, [ ].

If there is anything in the original that is a mistake or odd, for example a misspelling, and you want to make it clear that it really was like that, you can insert [sic]. *Sic* is Latin for 'so', or 'thus'.

For quotations within quotations, use double inverted commas. American practice is to use single inverted commas.

To separate the reported words, in inverted commas, from the reporting phrase, e.g. *she said*, use a comma, for example:

He said, 'Jane's not here.'

'Yes,' she said.

The comma comes before the inverted comma. Closing quotation marks follow the punctuation marks for the sentence of which they are part, except for a colon or semi-colon. See the previous example.

If you refer several times to something for which there is an established but not well known abbreviation, give the full form the first time you mention it, with the abbreviation in brackets after it. Subsequently, use the abbreviation alone.

For the preferred style for dates, see ◊dates.

3. Footnotes

Footnotes are pieces of extra information placed at the bottom of the page to which they relate. They were traditionally used to give information about the sources of material quoted or referred to in the main body of an essay or report. Current practice is to give at the end of the text a bibliography, that is, a list of books and articles consulted, and referred to in the text.

You can use footnotes for background or explanatory information hat might divert from the general line of argument if it were included in the text, but which some readers would be interested to look at. Some people prefer to keep the basic text free of the clutter of footnotes, and put the additional material in endnotes at the end of the text. Use footnotes and endnotes as little as possible, and keep them short. Use asterisks or superscript numbers in the text to indicate them.

A large block of information that would interrupt the text if included can be placed in a separate appendix at the end of the text.

4. Bibliographies

The last section of the essay or report is the bibliography, called the reference list in the USA. This is where you list the books and articles that you consulted when you were researching your subject and that might be useful to readers. They are listed in alphabetical order by authors' surnames. You need to give full details of each so that any reader who wishes to consult a copy may do so.

Each item in the bibliography should be set out consistently in a standard form. A common one has the elements in this order:

1 name(s) of the author(s), surname and comma before first name and initials
2 the title of the work
3 place of publication, publisher, and date of publication

Full stops are used at the end of each of these parts.

A large number of abbreviations are used in footnotes and bibliographies. Many are abbreviations for Latin words. Here is a list of the common ones, plus one or two Latin terms that are not abbreviated. The full Latin terms are given in italics.

c.	*circa*, about, approximately
cf.	*confer*, compare
cp.	compare
ed.	edited by
edit.	edition
e.g.	*exempli gratia*, for example
et al.	*et alii*, and others (used after the name of the first of several authors to save listing them all)
f.	following
fig.	figure
fl.	*floruit*, flourished (used with a date to say that a person was active then)
ib., ibid.	*ibidem*, in the same place, (i.e. in the last named reference)
i.e.	*id est*, that is (used to explain a term)
in loc. cit.	*in loco citato*, in the place cited (i.e. in the book or article to which you most recently referred)
l.	line (plural is ll.)
loc cit.	*loco citato*, in the place cited (i.e. in the book or article to which you most recently referred)
MS	manuscript (plural is MSS.)
op.cit.	*opere citato*, in the work cited (i.e. in the book or article to which you most recently referred)
p.	page (plural is pp.)
passim	here and there (used when a source is mentioned many times and in different parts of the text)
.q.v.	*quod vide*, which see
vid.	*vide*, see

et al See ♭etc.

etc This is an abbreviation of the Latin **et cetera**, meaning 'and other things'. Some people say that it should not be used with lists of people, or to mean 'and so forth' when referring to events or actions: *The children laughed, shouted, ran about, etc*. However, its use in these contexts is well established, although **et al** is more polite when referring to people (this is an abbreviation of the Latin *et alii*, meaning 'and others').

The more important question is whether you should use these abbreviations at all. They are useful for notes and on forms, but look out of place in ordinary writing; better to begin a list of examples with *such as* or *for example*, or to follow it with *and so on*, *and so forth*, or (with people) *and others*. Whatever form you use, make sure that you give some idea of what the other items might be.

In a sentence such as *there are worms etc in the garden*, **etc** could refer to almost anything: *worms, beetles, woodlice, and so on* suggests other creepy-crawlies, while: *creatures such as worms, spiders, and frogs* suggests a much wider range of wildlife. This means that you have to know what you mean: **etc** and its equivalents are often used when people are not sure, or cannot be bothered to think about, what they wish to include. Remember the **c** in *et cetera* is pronounced **s**. The *et* is sometimes incorrectly pronounced *ek*. Note also that **etc** and **et al** can be written with or without a full stop.

ethnic This is often used to mean 'foreign': *ethnic* clothing, fabrics, etc, being based (sometimes rather loosely) on the traditional materials and designs of other cultures, particularly peasant or tribal ones. Strictly speaking, this is incorrect, as *ethnic* refers to the combination of physical and cultural characteristics by which a group identifies itself or is identified by others, and everyone has some kind of ethnic background.

An *ethnic minority* is a group which is racially and culturally different from the majority of people in the society it belongs to; in the USA a member of such a group may be called *an ethnic*. Ethnicity is not the same as nationality; a person may be of British nationality (legally regarded as a British citizen), and ethnically Jewish, Welsh, Afro-Caribbean, Asian, etc. It also differs from race; Africans, Afro-Caribbeans and black Americans have common ancestry, but their history and culture have diverged, making them ethnically different.

evenness Remember that this word has two **ns**.

evince *or* **evoke** To **evince** something is to exhibit it or show that one has it: *Mozart evinced an amazing talent for music as a young child*. To **evoke** something is to bring it to mind or actually cause it as a response: *The music evoked memories of her days at school*; *The pianist's fine performance evoked prolonged applause from the audience*.

exacerbate The standard pronunciation is [igg-**zass**-erbate] with the stress on the second syllable, which rhymes with *lass*.

exaggerate Spelling: remember the two **gs** and one **r**.

exalt *or* **exult** To **exalt** someone or something is to raise them in esteem or honour by praising them: *Many of Churchill's contemporaries exalted him as a fine leader*; *''Tis not what man does which exalts him,* *but what man would do!'* (Robert Browning). To **exult** is to rejoice greatly: *Roberta exulted at her first professional success*; *'Exult O shores, and ring O bells!'* (Walt Whitman).

excellent Spelling: remember the **c**.

except See ▷accept.

exception proves the rule, the This is often used to mean that the exception confirms the rule. However, *prove* in this case means 'test'; the fact that there is an exception implies that the rule may not be valid, or may need some modification. The phrase is perhaps most often used as a more or less meaningless reply to an inconvenient fact: *'You're always late'. 'I was early this morning'. 'Ah, but the exception proves the rule!'*.

exceptional *or* **exceptionable** **Exceptional** refers to something that forms an exception, usually with the implication that it is especially good or important: *The book was of exceptional interest to those who had shared the writer's experiences*; *Marian's gift for gardening is exceptional*. **Exceptionable** means that a thing is open to objection, that is, people take exception to it: *We referred him to a child psychiatrist because of his continuing exceptionable behaviour*.

exciting Spelling: remember the **c**.

exclamation mark *or* **exclamation point** This is a punctuation mark (!) used to indicate emphasis or strong emotion: *That's terrible!*. It is appropriate after interjections: *Rats!*, emphatic greetings: *Yo!*, and orders: *Shut up!*, as well as those sentences beginning *How* or *What* that are not questions: *How embarrassing!; What a surprise!*.

The exclamation mark is most often seen in dialogue. Its use is kept to a minimum in narrative prose and technical writing. Within a quotation an exclamation mark may be placed in square brackets to indicate that the writer or editor is surprised by something.

Exclamation marks are used to indicate urgency; contrast *Let me get out, I need to go home* with *Let me out! I'm choking in here!* They are sometimes used to suggest heavy sarcasm: *You are a great goalkeeper!* means the opposite in the context of a lost game. Overuse of exclamation marks reduces their impact. Double exclamation marks are always to be avoided.

exercise *or* **exorcize** To **exercise** is to use or practise the mind or body in some activity: *Jogging exercises the body and often the mind as* *well.* To **exorcize** something is to drive it out, with particular reference to an evil spirit: *The minister exorcized the house when the family claimed they had an active poltergeist.* The words are unrelated.

expatriate Spelling: remember that the ending is **-ate**, not **-ot**.

explicable The standard pronunciation is [ix-**plick**-able], but traditionalists maintain that the word should be pronounced [ex-plickable] with the stress on the first syllable.

extraordinary Spelling: remember **extra** plus **ordinary**.

extrovert Spelling: remember the **o**, not an **a** in the middle.

exult See ▷exalt.

facia *or* **fascia** This word can be spelled either way.

Fahrenheit Spelling: note the **ei**.

faint *or* **feint** Use **faint** when referring to dizziness, a loss of consciousness, or swooning. Use **feint** when you mean a pretended punch in boxing. Either spelling can be used to describe fine rules on paper, although *feint* is more common.

famous *or* **infamous** A **famous** person or deed is widely known and is usually good or praiseworthy: *We saw a film about Captain Scott, the famous explorer.* An **infamous** person or deed is widely known and is bad or to be deplored: *We saw a film about the infamous king Richard III.*

farther *or* **further** Both have the same meaning, but **farther** is used only when referring to physical distance: *He lives farther* (or further) *from the station than I do.* **Further** can also be used to mean 'additional' or 'to a greater extent or degree': *Since we last spoke there have been further developments*; *I intend to take this matter further.*

fascia See ◊facia.

fascinating Spelling: remember the **sc**.

fascism Spelling: remember the **sc** (also in *fascist*).

fashion Spelling: remember the **i**.

fatal *or* **fateful** If something is **fatal** it causes death: *His second heart attack was fatal.* If it is **fateful** it is ominous or decisive, perhaps bringing death, but perhaps not: *That day was to be the fateful one for her.* In popular speech, however, the two words are not differentiated: *Have you seen the gory film* Fatal Attraction?

faze Faze, meaning 'daunt', 'perturb', 'disconcert', is usually used in negative statements: *Nothing fazes her.* It comes from the USA and Canada, and is still regarded as an Americanism. However, it is a useful word and is slowly becoming accepted. Avoid using it in formal contexts.

feasible Spelling: remember the ending **-ible**.

February Spelling: remember the **br**.

feign Spelling: note the **ei** and the **g**.

feint See ◊faint.

feisty This is an Americanism which is gaining ground in British and Australian English. It is defined in many dictionaries as 'aggressive, excitable, nervous, touchy' but is now more often used to mean 'spirited', 'assertive', 'able to speak up for oneself' (usually applied to women). It has also appeared in an advertisement for a high-performance car, presumably suggesting that the car is fast, tough, and exciting to drive.

Words tend to change their meanings with time, sometimes through an error which gradually becomes accepted (as with *decimate*), often by being applied to different things, as in this case. *Feisty* is changing too quickly for dictionaries to keep up with – and it remains to be seen what the accepted meaning will eventually be.

ferment See ◊foment.

fervent *or* **fervid** Something **fervent** is warm or passionate: *It is my fervent wish that we shall all meet again very soon*. **Fervid** has the same sense, but is a more literary word and carries something of a greater strength: *The soldier was welcomed home amid fervid excitement*.

fewer *or* **less** Fewer means 'not so many'; **less** means 'not so much': *Fewer jobs mean less money in the town*; *Fewer people would take up less room*. *Less* is used with expressions of quantity: *less than five miles*; *less than 10*. *Less* is often used in place of *fewer*, but this is widely regarded as incorrect and should be avoided, especially in formal writing.

fiancé *or* **fiancée** Use **fiancé** for a man, and **fiancée** for a woman.

fifth Spelling: remember the second **f** (also in *fifthly*).

filament Spelling: note the single **l**.

filthiness Spelling: the **y** in *filthy* changes to an **i**.

finally Spelling: remember the double **l**.

finance In Britain the pronunciation for the noun: *Finance is going to be a problem*) is [**fye**-nance], although [fye-**nance**] is also common. The verb: *The dam has been financed by the British government* is usually [fye-**nance**]. The US pronunciations are the other way round.

fiord *or* **fjord** This word can be spelled either way.

first *or* **firstly** Either can be used to begin a list, or to introduce a series of questions or statements: *I have two questions. First, do we need it? Second, can we afford it?*; *Firstly, we must have it. Secondly, we've got plenty of money.* Whichever you choose, be consistent: **first** should be followed by *second, third*, **firstly** by *secondly, thirdly*, and so on.

fizziness Spelling: the **y** in *fizzy* changes to an **i**.

fjord See ◊fiord.

flaccid The recommended pronunciation used to be [**flack**-sid], but the pronunciation that rhymes with *acid* is now commonly accepted.

flagrant See ◊blatant.

flammable See ◊inflammable.

flaunt See ◊flout.

fleshly *or* **fleshy** Both adjectives relate to flesh, but **fleshly** relates to 'the' flesh, that is the body, with its sensual and sexual connotations: *'Abstain from fleshly lusts, which war against the soul'* (Bible: 1 Peter 2.11). **Fleshy** thus usually relates to the physical qualities of flesh, such as its plumpness, softness, or colour: *She had fleshy arms and even fleshier thighs*; *There's nothing I like more than a nice fleshy peach.*

floatation *or* **flotation** This word can be spelled either way, although the second spelling is more common.

floor In Britain, the *first floor* is above the *ground floor*, which is at street level. In the USA the *first floor* is at street level, with the *second floor* corresponding to the British *first floor*.

flotation See ◊floatation.

flotsam *or* **jetsam** Technically, **flotsam** is cargo or wreckage floating on the surface of the sea, while **jetsam** is cargo that has been thrown overboard (jettisoned) or washed up on the beach. However, the two words are linked to refer to homeless people: *The government seemed to do little to help the flotsam and jetsam of society.*

flounder *or* **founder** To **flounder** is to struggle in an attempt to retain control in a situation: *The swimmer began to flounder in the heavy seas*; *My next question made him flounder.* To **founder** is to sink or collapse: *The ship sprang a leak and started to founder*; *The project foundered when we no longer had the funds to support it.*

flout *or* **flaunt** To **flout** someone or something is to treat them with contempt and ignore them: *The school's lack of discipline meant that* *many pupils flouted the rules*. To **flaunt** something is to parade it ostentatiously: *He loved flaunting his knowledge on the subject*. People sometimes use *flaunt* when they mean 'flout' so use these words with care.

fogginess Spelling: the **y** in *foggy* changes to an **i**.

foment *or* **ferment** To **foment** is to stir up trouble or something undesirable: *I don't want to foment any ill feeling*. To **ferment** is to stir up emotions or reactions, not necessarily bad ones: *The race fermented considerable excitement among the spectators*.

for- *or* **fore-** Words beginning **for-** have the idea of doing without or forbidding in their meaning, while words beginning **fore-** have the idea of going before or into the future in their meaning. Note especially the spellings of these words:

forbear (abstain); forbid; forgo (do without); forebear (ancestor); forecast; foregoing (preceding); foretell

forbid *or* **prohibit** Both mean to state, from a position of authority, that someone must not do something, or that something must not be done: *Parents should forbid their children to smoke*. **Prohibit** means to make the act illegal: *The government has prohibited the sale of cigarettes to children*. The past tense of **forbid** is either *forbad* or *forbade*; *forbidden* is the past participle.

foreign Spelling: note the **ei**.

foresee Spelling: remember the **e** after the **r**.

foreword *or* **forward** remember that **forward** means near or towards the front. A **foreword** is an introduction to a book.

forfeit Spelling: note the **ei**.

formally See ◊*formerly*.

former, latter **Former** refers to the first of two things, **latter** to the second. Strictly speaking, if there are more than two things *first* or *first-named* and *last* or *last-named* should be used, but this rule is often ignored. The use of *former* and *latter* mean that the reader has to go back over the sentence (or, worse, the listener has to remember it). It is usually better to repeat a word; in the sentence *Some people prefer dogs to cats because the former are more faithful* it is easier, and kinder to the reader, to write *because dogs are more faithful*.

formerly *or* **formally** The words are unrelated but sound exactly the same and often make sense even when one is misused in place of the other. **Formerly** means previously, earlier: *Agreement was formerly given* (it was given earlier); **formally** means in a formal manner: *Agreement was formally given* (it was given officially or in principle).

formidable Although a majority of British speakers probably stress the second syllable, the pronunciation with the stress on the first syllable has more prestige. Americans usually place the stress on the first syllable.

fortuitous This is sometimes used instead of *fortunate*. It means 'by chance', 'accidentally', whether that chance is fortunate or not.

forty Spelling: remember that there is no **u**.

forward See ▷foreword.

founder See ▷flounder.

Frances *or* **Francis** **Frances** is the feminine form of the name, **Francis** is the masculine form, often shortened to *Frank*.

freight Spelling: note the **ei**.

friend Spelling: remember it is **ie**.

friendliness Spelling: the **y** of *friendly* changes to an **i**.

frigid Spelling: note that there is no **d** before the **g**.

friskiness Spelling: the **y** of *frisky* changes to an **i**.

frolic Spelling: note that there is no **k** (but remember *frolicked* and *frolicking*).

fruitiness Spelling: the **y** of *fruity* changes to an **i**.

fuchsia Spelling: remember that the plant was named after a botanist called Leonard Fuchs.

-ful *or* **-full** See ▷spelling rules.

fulfil Spelling: note the two single **l**s.

full stop This is a punctuation mark (.) used to indicate the end of a sentence or an abbreviation.

The use of a comma where a full stop or at least a semicolon is needed has been the most common error in written English for many years. Commas would be inadequate to punctuate this piece: *I looked at my watch it was five o'clock in the morning this was always a dangerous time we had the dawn at our backs the enemy would see us outlined against the sky.*

There are five complete statements here. Each may be a sentence marked by full stops and capital letters. Since the statements are closely linked, this would be an opportunity to use semicolons. But commas do not provide a sufficiently strong pause. They are not traditionally the marks used for separating complete statements.

There are no fixed rules about the use of full stops to indicate abbreviations, but the growing practice is to omit them: *Mr* rather than *Mr., Cambs* rather than *Cambs..*

A comma can be used after an abbreviation that has a full stop: *Fred Smith, M.P., O.B.E., said...,* but if it falls at the end of a sentence, only one full stop is used: *He was awarded the O.B.E.* not *He was awarded the O.B.E..*

fulsome Fulsome praise or thanks are not just given wholeheartedly and enthusiastically, they are laid on with a trowel. In modern English **fulsome** is derogatory, meaning 'too effusive or flattering', 'overdone'.

fungous *or* fungus Remember that **fungous** is the adjective and **fungus** is the noun.

funniness Spelling: the **y** of *funny* changes to an **i**.

further See ◊farther.

fussiness Spelling: the **y** of *fussy* changes to an **i**.

fuzziness Spelling: the **y** of *fuzzy* changes to an **i**.

Gaelic *or* **Gallic** **Gaelic** relates to the Celtic languages of the people of Scotland and Ireland: *The Gaelic languages are closely related.* **Gallic** relates to the Gauls, the ancestors of the French, or to the French themselves: *Our French hosts were Gallic charm personified.*

The most common pronunciation of *Gaelic* is [**gay**-lick], but [**gal**-ick], beginning like *gallon*, is also acceptable.

gaiety Spelling: note the **e**.

gala Two pronunciations are heard, [**gar**-ler] and [**gay**-ler]. Americans use the latter.

Gallic See ◊Gaelic.

gamble *or* **gambol** To **gamble** is to risk or chance something: *He gambled away a lot of his money on the pools*; *I wouldn't gamble on the weather staying fine.* To **gambol** is to frisk or leap about playfully: *The little lambs were gambolling in the field*; *After the wedding the younger children were gambolling around the churchyard.*

gambol See ◊gamble.

gaol *or* **jail** This word can be spelled either way, although American English uses **jail**. (Note also **gaoler** and **jailer**).

garage There are several alternative pronunciations in British English: [**ga**-raj, **ga**-rardge, **ga**- ridge], the last one being regarded by some as non-standard. Americans put the stress on the second syllable [g'-**raj**, g'-**rardge**].

gaseous In British English *gaseous* does not have the same vowel as *gas*, but is pronounced [**gay**- seous]. The US pronunciation is [**gash**-ous].

gauge Spelling: note the **au**.

gay The most common meaning of **gay** in everyday use is now 'homosexual'. Many people regret the loss of the older meanings 'jolly', 'merry', 'bright', 'colourful'; they can still be used, but only with great care when there is no possible ambiguity. As a noun, *gay* usually refers to a man. Many homosexual women prefer the older term *lesbian*, although some will use *gay* as an adjective: *I'm a lesbian; I'm gay*. Gay people may use *queer* among themselves, but regard its use by heterosexuals as offensive.

genealogy Spelling: note the **a** in the middle, not an **o**.

gerund A gerund, or verbal noun, is a form of a verb with an *-ing* ending which has some of the characteristics of a noun. For example, it can be the object of a verb: *The council has decided to ban smoking in its offices* or the subject of a verb: *Smoking is strictly forbidden*. But it can also retain some characteristics of a verb – for instance, if its base verb is transitive, a gerund can take an object: *Smoking a pipe is supposed to be less harmful than smoking cigarettes*. Nouns formed from verbs with *-ing* that are pluralizable, like *etching*, as in *Come up and see my etchings*, are not classified as gerunds.

In traditional grammar, any pronoun or noun that precedes a gerund should be in the possessive case: *I disapprove of his smoking*; *I resented Sarah's taking my place*. In practice, though, in present-day English most people use the object form of pronouns: *I disapprove of him smoking* and do not inflect nouns: *I resented Sarah taking my place*. This usage (which is sometimes termed a *fused participle*) is perfectly acceptable in standard English, and indeed it is probably preferable to using possessive forms, which can sound stilted and cumbersome.

geyser In the usual British pronunciation *gey-* rhymes with *key*. A few people use the pronunciation [guy] for the 'hot spring' meaning. This is the usual pronunciation in the USA.

gherkin Spelling: remember the **h**.

gibe, gybe, *or* **jibe** To gibe someone, or at someone, is to mock them or jeer at them: *They gibed him about the error*. To **gybe**, as applied to a sailing ship, is to shift direction: *The yacht gybed suddenly to port*. Both verbs have the alternative spelling **jibe**.

gill The word for the liquid measure is pronounced [jill]. The word for other meanings (as in fish or mushroom) is pronounced [gill] with a hard **g** like *go*.

gipsy *or* **gypsy** This word can be spelled either way.

girl Girl, as an informal word for *woman* (the female equivalent of 'chap', 'bloke', 'guy,' etc) should be used with great care. Many adult women object strongly to being called *girls* by men. A man who refers to his female secretary as *my girl* will almost certainly cause offence, as will a sports commentator who says (however truthfully), *In cricket the girls' team generally does better than the men's.*

A woman may refer to another woman as a girl, particularly if they have known each other since they were girls or if the other woman is younger. A woman may also call the female members of a group that she belongs to *the girls*. A man might get away with this if it is clear that no offence is intended, but it is safer for him to refer to them as *the ladies*. See also ▷lady.

glamorous Spelling: note that there is no **u** before the **r** as there is in *glamour*.

glisten Spelling: remember the **t**.

goddess Spelling: note the double **d**.

gourmand *or* **gourmet** A **gourmand** is someone who is excessively fond of food and drink: *He's a real gourmand, and never stints on his weekly shopping.* A **gourmet** is a connoisseur of food and drink: *TV cookery expert Graham Kerr was nicknamed the 'Galloping Gourmet' because he produced exquisite dishes with lightning speed.* Remember the **u** when spelling these two words.

government Spelling: remember the first **n**.

graceful *or* **gracious** A **graceful** person or thing shows grace or elegance: *The ballet dancer gave a graceful leap across the stage.* A **gracious** person or thing is kindly or indulgent, as typically aristocrats and royalty are or were said to be: *Gracious living is not everyone's cup of tea.* The word can be used patronisingly or sarcastically: *How incredibly decent of you to honour us with your gracious presence.*

graffiti This is actually a plural, but the singular form *graffito* is seldom used. Strictly speaking, *graffiti* should be treated as a plural and followed by a plural verb, although is more often seen with a singular verb: *Graffiti is an eyesore.* To refer to a single item, use *piece* or *bit of*: *I saw a good bit of graffiti today.*

grammar Spelling: remember the ending **-ar** not **-er**.

grand- *or* **great-** In family relationships, **grand-** is used for one's parents' parents and for one's children's children, while **great-** is used for one's grandparents' parents and one's grandchildren's children: *My* *grandfather was born in London and his father, my great-grandfather, in Reading*. For relatives by marriage one can use *great-* or *grand-*, but *great-* is always more common: *He had a surprise visit from his great-niece*; *She has kept in touch with her grand-aunt*.

grandad *or* **granddad** This word can be spelled either way, although *grandad* is more common.

granddaughter Spelling: remember the two **d**s.

great- See ◊grand-.

Great Britain See ◊Britain.

greengrocer's apostrophe See ◊apostrophe.

Greenwich The most common pronunciation of the name of the London borough, the meridian, Greenwich village in New York, and the town in Connecticut is [**Gren**-itch]. Pronunciation of the first syllable as [grin] and of the last syllable as [idge] is also heard both in Britain and the USA.

grey US spelling: *gray*.

grievance Spelling: note the **ie**.

grisly *or* **grizzly** When writing these words, use **grisly** to mean horrible and **grizzly** to mean a bear.

guarantee Spelling: remember the **u**.

guerrilla This word, meaning 'fighter', is easy to misspell. Remember the **u** and the double **r** and double **l**. *Guerilla* is an alternative spelling.

guitar Spelling: remember the **u**.

gybe See ◊gibe.

gypsy See ◊gipsy.

haemorrhage Spelling: remember the double **r** and the **h**. In American English it is spelled *hemorrhage*.

hairiness Spelling: the **y** of *hairy* changes to an **i**.

half *Half is* or *half are*? The answer depends entirely on what comes after *half*. If it is a singular noun, use a singular verb: *Half (of) the town was in darkness after the power failure*. If it is a plural noun, use a plural verb: *Half (of) the members want to change the rules*. If it is a collective singular, you can use a singular verb or a plural verb: *Half (of) the party supports/support the call for a ballot*.

handicraft Spelling: note the **i**.

handkerchief Spelling: remember the **d**.

hanged *or* **hung** **Hung** is the usual form of the past tense and past participle of the verb *to hang*. **Hanged** is used only in the sense 'kill by hanging': *He hanged himself with a rope hung from a beam*.

happiness Spelling: the **y** of *happy* changes to an **i**.

harass The traditional British pronunciation is [**harr**-us] with the stress on the first syllable, but in the 1970s the American [h'-**rass**] with a weaker first syllable began to be heard, and has since become very common, to the annoyance of some who keep to the traditional British pronunciation.

harassment Spelling: remember it has one **r** and two **ss**.

hasten Spelling: note the **t**.

haughtiness Spelling: the **y** of *haughty* changes to an **i**.

have *or* **have got** In everyday British English speech **have got** is used to show possession: *I've got twenty pounds*. In American English and in more formal British English **have** is used alone: *I have only five*. In formal British English, questions and negative statements use *have*: '*Have you enough money?*' '*No, I have not*'. In American English **do have** is used: '*Do you have enough money?* 'No, I don't' or 'No, I don't have any*'.

Haydn The name of the composer is pronounced [**hide**-n]. The Welsh name is pronounced [**hade**-n].

haziness Spelling: the **y** of *hazy* changes to an **i**.

he/she/they After certain indefinite pronouns, such as *anyone* and *neither*, it is traditional in standard English to use the masculine singular pronouns *he, him* and *his*. However, it is increasingly being seen as invidious to implicitly exclude women and girls by using *he* rather than *she*, and *they* is now widely used instead. To find out more about this, see ◊they/their/theirs.

healthiness Spelling: the **y** of *healthy* changes to an **i**.

heartiness Spelling: the **y** of *hearty* changes to an **i**.

heaviness Spelling: the **y** of *heavy* changes to an **i**.

hegemony The main British pronunciation has a hard **g** as in *go* [hig-**ghem**-uh-ny], though alternative pronunciations with a soft **g** or with the stress on the first syllable are also heard. The standard US pronunciation has a soft **g** [huh-**jem**-uh-ny].

heifer Spelling: note the **ei**.

height Spelling: note the **ei**.

heinous The standard pronunciation is [**hay**-nus]. The pronunciation [**hee**-nus] is regarded as non-standard. A pronunciation that rhymes with *genius* is probably based on the mistaken idea that there is an **i** in the spelling of the second syllable. Spelling: note the **ei**.

heir Spelling: note the **ei**. (Two related words are *heirloom* and *heiress*).

hence This means 'from here'; there is no need to use *from* before it. The same is true of *thence* 'from there' and *whence* 'from where'.

heroin *or* **heroine** Remember that **heroin** is the drug and **heroine** is the female hero.

heyday Spelling: note that it is **hey**, not **hay**.

hiccup *or* **hiccough** This word can be spelled either way.

Hilary This name can be used for both sexes, with no difference in spelling.

Hindi *or* **Hindu** Many people are confused by these terms. **Hindi** is a language derived from Sanskrit. A dialect of it is the main language of Indian literature and one of the official languages of India. Another dialect, *Hindustani*, is spoken in Delhi and used as a common language throughout India. A **Hindu** is a follower of Hinduism, the main religion of India.

historic *or* **historical** A **historic** event is an important one, or one that may come to be regarded as important: *The two heads of state signed a historic agreement*. A **historical** event is one that belongs to history, so that it actually took place: *King Arthur is generally believed to be a historical figure, though some regard him as legendary*.

hitchhike Spelling: note the double **h**.

hoard *or* **horde** A **hoard** is a store or accumulation of things: *An important hoard of Roman coins was found in a field in Suffolk*. A **horde** is a large group of people: *There were hordes of bargain hunters at the sales*.

hoi polloi A few people still insist that, as the literal translation of this Greek phrase is 'the many', you should not use *the* in front of it. However, no one says *the polloi*, which would be a logical application of the rule. **Hoi polloi** has been adopted into English and need not be treated as a Greek phrase: in English usage *the hoi polloi* is quite correct.

Holborn The **l** is not pronounced in this name of a part of London. The pronunciation is [**hoe**-b'n].

holiness Spelling: the **y** in *holy* changes to an **i**.

holy See ▷wholly.

homage Spelling: note the single **m**.

homeliness Spelling: the **y** in *homely* changes to an **i**.

homogeneous *or* **homogenous** Homogeneous means 'the same throughout', 'made of the same substance': *The Christian church is not a homogeneous body; it has room for many shades of opinion*. **Homogenous** can also have this meaning, but it is more often used in a technical sense, 'corresponding in parts or organs, owing to similar ancestry or evolutionary adaptation'.

homosexual Both [home] and [hom] are accepted pronunciations of the first syllable. [Home] is probably more common, but purists prefer [hom] on the grounds that it is closer to the pronunciation of the Greek source. In the USA only the [home] pronunciation is heard.

hopefully Most people now accept the use of **hopefully** to mean 'it is hoped (that)'. In this sense it is separated from the rest of the sentence by commas, and often comes before the part it refers to: *They are saving hopefully to buy a house* means that they are saving their money in a spirit of hope, looking forward to their own home; *hopefully, they are saving*, or *they are saving, hopefully, to buy a house* means that the speaker hopes that they intend to use the money to buy a house, and not for some other purpose.

horde See ◊hoard.

horrific Spelling: remember the double **r** and single **f**.

houmous *or* **houmus** This word, meaning 'chickpea paste', can be spelled either way. The stress is on the first syllable, which rhymes with *room*, or sometimes *broom*. The second syllable is like the end of *famous*. Do not confuse it with *humus*, which means 'decomposed matter in soil' and is pronounced [**hyoo**-mous].

humerus This word, meaning a bone in the upper arm, must not be confused with ◊humorous.

humorous This word, meaning funny, is easy to misspell. Note that there is no **u** before the **r** as there is in *humour*.

humus See ◊houmous.

hygiene Spelling: remember the **i**.

hypercritical See ◊hypocrite.

hyphen This is a punctuation mark (-) used in forming compound words and to indicate a word break at the end of a line.

Not all compound words are hyphenated, but the hyphen is needed to link adjectives that jointly qualify a noun or nouns: *red-hot poker*; *Mrs Brown's twenty-odd nephews and nieces*. Without the hyphen, the adjectives would apply separately to the nouns: a poker red in colour and hot, nephews and nieces twenty in number and odd in character.

Some compounds contain more than one hyphen: *mother-in-law*; *up-to-date*. There are no definite rules about when to hyphenate compound nouns. For example, you could write worldview, world view, or worldview. Generally, the more closely associated the words become, the more appropriate it is to merge them. A hyphen may be considered a middle way between separation and complete integration, but the modern tendency is to use fewer hyphens in compound words.

A hyphen is also used to mark a word break at the end of a line, to avoid a space or an ugly squashing-in.

hypocrisy Spelling: note the ending -**sy**, not -**cy**.

hypocrite Spelling: remember the **y**, and note that it has an **o** in the middle, not **er**. Do not confuse the adjective *hypocritical* with *hypercritical*, which means 'overly critical'.

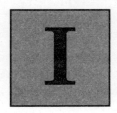

I/me; we/us; you Compound objects containing pronouns are in the accusative case in standard English, not the nominative case, so *between you and me* is acceptable but *between you and I* is not. To find out more about this, see ▷between you and me.

-ible *or* **-able** See ▷spelling rules.

iciness Spelling: the **y** of *icy* changes to an **i**.

icon *or* **ikon** This word can be spelled either way.

idiosyncrasy Spelling: remember the second **i**, the **y** in the middle, and the ending **-asy**.

idyllic Spelling: remember the **y**.

ikon See ▷icon.

ilk This is a Scots word, meaning 'same', used when the name of a property is the same as that of its owner: *the Knockwinnocks of that ilk* are the Knockwinnock family who own or live at Knockwinnock. It is often used to mean 'of the same name or family' or 'of the same type': *The Davises are a family of engineers, and one of that ilk designs oil tankers*; *Barbara Cartland and her ilk* (other writers of romantic fiction). Strictly speaking this is incorrect, and some Scots object to it quite strongly.

illegal *or* **illicit** Something **illegal** is forbidden by law: *It is illegal for motorcyclists not to wear a crash helmet*. If a thing is **illicit** it is done by someone who knows that it is disallowed by law but that under different circumstances it could be legal: *The crew were involved in the illicit import of brandy* (it is basically legal to import brandy but not the way they did it).

illusion See ▷delusion.

immaculate Spelling: remember the double **m**.

immediately Spelling: remember the double **m**.

immigrant Spelling: remember the double **m**.

imminent Spelling: remember **-ent**, not **-ant**.

immoral *or* **amoral** An **immoral** person or thing has low or corrupt moral standards: *She lived on her immoral earnings as a prostitute*; *Some might find that book immoral.* An **amoral** person or thing has no moral standards: *Some tribes were known to be quite amoral, with no sense of right or wrong.* Spelling: *immoral*, remember the double **m**.

impact Many people dislike **impact** used as a verb: *The spacecraft has impacted on Mars*; *The new taxes will impact on young families.* It is easy to avoid it by using *hit, strike,* or *effect. Have an impact* (i.e. an effect) is rather overused; *effect* or *have an effect* are alternatives.

Although these phrases are often used negatively, they are neutral: *The single market will have an effect* (or an impact) *on our business* means that the business will change, but does not say whether the change will be for the better or the worse.

impetuous See ◊compulsive.

imply *or* **infer** These are often confused. Both concern information which is not expressed directly. **Imply** refers to the source of the information: *He didn't actually say I took the money, but he implied it; Her repeated absences from class imply a lack of interest in the subject.* **Infer** refers to gaining information indirectly by working it out: *From what he said everyone inferred that I took the money; I think we can infer from her repeated absences that she is not really interested in the subject.*

impresario Spelling: note the single **s**.

impulsive See ◊compulsive.

in behalf of See ◊behalf.

inapt See ◊inept.

incredible *or* **incredulous** **Incredible** is used of something unbelievable or difficult to believe; **incredulous** is used of someone who is disbelieving: *When he described his incredible escape, she listened with an increasingly incredulous expression.* Compare ◊credible.

incurred Spelling: note the double **r** (unlike *incur*).

indebted Spelling: remember the **b**.

indefinite article See ◊article.

indefinite pronoun a pronoun that does not refer to or replace a specific noun. *Anybody, nobody, one, none, some*, and *anything* are examples of indefinite pronouns.

independent Spelling: remember the ending **-ent**, not **-ant**.

Indian Many people from Bangladesh, Pakistan, and Sri Lanka dislike being referred to as *Indian*. (The correct adjectives are *Bangladeshi, Pakistani,* and *Sri Lankan. Paki* is offensive, even if the person is from Pakistan.) *Asian* is acceptable but vague; *from the Indian subcontinent* longer but more accurate.

   Some of the indigenous peoples of the Americas, particularly North America, would rather be called *Native American*, although *American Indian* is usually acceptable: **Indian** by itself is ambiguous, *Red Indian* is offensive. The indigenous peoples of the extreme north of Canada, commonly called *Eskimos* although they prefer the term *Inuit*, are often included in the term *Native American*: many of them object.

indictment Note the silent **c**. The word is pronounced [in-**dite**-ment].

indigenous Spelling: note the **e**.

indispensable Spelling: note the ending **-able**.

ineffectual *or* **ineffective** Something that is **ineffective** does not produce the desired effect or results: *He complained that the hair-restoring lotion had been quite ineffective.* **Ineffectual** can mean this, but is also used of a thing or person that is incapable of doing what is necessary: *She made an ineffectual attempt to get rid of the fly.* See also ◊effective.

inept *or* **inapt** An **inept** remark is an absurd or clumsy one: *He said a few inept words by way of an introduction* (they were not well chosen). An **inapt** remark is an inappropriate one: *He mumbled an inapt apology* (it was not adequate for the occasion).

inequity *or* **iniquity** **Inequity** is unfairness or injustice: *Some members grumbled about the inequity of the voting system.* **Iniquity** is wickedness or immorality: *The newspaper columnist wrote a powerful piece condemning the iniquity of the government; The disco was said by some to be a den of iniquity, with alcohol and drugs freely available.*

infamous This is not pronounced to rhyme with *famous*. The stress is on the first syllable, and the other two vowels are weak [**inn**-fermus]. See also ◊famous.

infectious *or* **contagious** In medical terms, an **infectious** disease is one spread by germs: *Typhoid and typhus are both highly infectious diseases.* In figurative terms, the word is used of something irresistibly catching: *Her infectious laughter brightened the meal.*

Medically, **contagious** is used of a disease spread by bodily contact: *Scarlet fever is a contagious disease formerly known as scarlatina.* Figuratively, the word is used of something that spreads rapidly: *His enthusiasm for the project was contagious, and we soon joined in.*

infer See ◊imply.

infinitive The basic form of a verb, the form by which verbs are identified: *to be; to hit; to love* and so on. The infinitive form of the verb in English is always preceded by *to*. See also ◊split infinitive.

inflammable Inflammable means the same as *flammable*, 'liable to catch fire', 'easily ignited'. Because it is often taken to mean the opposite, it is best to avoid using it at all; in official use *flammable* and *non-flammable* are the preferred terms.

inflection A word ending that indicates the word's function in the sentence. Examples of inflections are *-ed* in *posted*, *-s* in *girls*, and *-est* in *longest*.

ingenious, ingenuous, *or* **disingenuous** Ingenious is used of something done with ingenuity, that is, cleverly or enterprisingly: *Sally had an ingenious method of keeping the bread fresh.* **Ingenuous** applies to something done innocently or artlessly: *Timmy's an ingenuous child: he asked if the eggs were the same colour as the chicken that laid them.* **Disingenuous** means devious or dishonest, or pretending to be *ingenuous*: *She's being rather disingenuous, telling you that her car has nothing wrong with it.*

inhuman *or* **inhumane** Somebody or something **inhuman** lacks normal human qualities such as kindness and pity: *It was inhuman to take the child away from her parents like that.* An **inhumane** person or thing is cruel, and insensitive to the suffering of others: *Many people are concerned about the inhumane treatment of animals.*

iniquity See ◊inequity.

innate Spelling: remember the double **n**.

innocuous Spelling: remember the double **n**.

innovate Spelling: remember the double **n**, and the **o**, not **er**.

innumerable See ◊numerous.

inoculation Spelling: remember it has only one **n** at the beginning.

inquire See ◊enquire.

inseparable Spelling: remember -**par**-, not -**per**-.

insidious *or* **invidious** Something **insidious** is gradually and stealthily harmful or destructive: *Cancer is often an insidious disease*; *His constant criticism had an insidious effect on morale and goodwill.* Something **invidious** causes resentment or unpopularity, especially if it is seen to be unfair: *Teachers are often faced with invidious duties*; *You have put me in an invidious position, and I am tempted to refuse.*

install Spelling: note the double **l** but remember *instalment*. US spelling: *installment*.

instant *or* **instantaneous** If something is **instant** it happens immediately, at once: *Any employee who broke this ruling was faced with instant dismissal.* Something **instantaneous** also happens immediately, but often as a consequence of something else, that is, at the instant of its occurrence: *Death was instantaneous* (at the moment of the accident or heart attack which caused it).

instil Spelling: note the single **l** (but remember *instilled* and *instilling*). US spelling: *instill*.

insure See ♭assure.

intense *or* **intensive** If something is **intense** it is great or powerful: *The heat was intense*; *I was filled with intense curiosity.* If it is **intensive** it is concentrated: *The city was subjected to intensive bombardment*; *The course was an intensive one, with little free time and frequent tests.*

intercede Spelling: note the ending -**cede**, not -**sede**.

interface This means a surface where two spaces or bodies meet: *the interface of air and water.* In recent years it has come to be used for an apparatus that connects two devices or systems so that they can work together; in the language of information technology, a device which enables a user to communicate with a computer, or computers to communicate with each other. In this sense *interface* is also a verb: *This machine will interface with most PCs.*

Figuratively, *interface* can refer to almost any boundary: *Design is at the interface of art and technology.* As a verb it is used to mean 'combine or cooperate with': *Your job will be to interface with the marketing department.* This sounds like jargon. Before using *interface* figuratively, ask yourself whether you need to; words such as *boundary, border, meeting-place, combine, work with, cooperate* will often express the sense just as well.

interment *or* **internment** Interment is the burial of a corpse: *The interment will take place immediately after the service.* **Internment** is the imprisonment or confinement, without trial, of an enemy or terrorist: *The internment of suspected terrorists was in force in Northern Ireland in the early 1970s.*

interrelated Spelling: note the double **r**.

intransitive verb A verb that cannot have an object noun or pronoun after it, such as *wait; happen.* A verb that is followed by an object is a transitive verb. Some verbs can be transitive or intransitive.

introvert Spelling: note the **o**, not **a**.

inveigle The standard pronunciation is [in-**vay**- gle] but [in-**vee**-gle] is also acceptable.

inventory This word is stressed on the first syllable [**in**-vuhn-tree], not on the second. The ending is pronounced [tree] in British English and [tory] in American English.

invidious See ◊insidious.

invigorate See ◊enervate.

ironic In drama, *irony* is the dramatic effect produced when the audience knows more than the characters in the play. In everyday use, an **ironic** remark is one, often humorous, that means the opposite of what is said, particularly if it appears to be sincere: *You're every bit as good as your brother* is ironic if the speaker thinks the listener's brother is no good at all. *Ironic* is often used loosely to mean paradoxical, the opposite of what might be expected: *Ironically, the poorest people are often the most generous.* Although this usage is fairly well established, some people dislike it. Consider whether you really need anything to introduce the statement. If you do, *paradoxically, strangely, oddly enough* etc can be used. Avoid using *ironic* to mean simply odd, unexpected, out of the ordinary.

irradiate Spelling: note the double **r**.

irregular Spelling: note the double **r**.

irrelevant Spelling: note the double **r**.

irrespective *or* **regardless** These have almost the same meaning, but are grammatically different. **Irrespective** is a preposition, used when something is not affected by the factors named: *Drunken driving is* *wrong, irrespective of the consequences*; *the job is open to all, irrespective of age*. **Regardless** is an adverb, and is used when someone acts, treating the factors named as unimportant: *She carried on, regardless of the pain*. The existence of two such similar terms has given rise to the hybrid *irregardless*. This is not generally accepted; it should never be used in formal contexts and is best not used at all.

irrupt See ▷erupt.

-ise *or* **-ize** See ▷spelling rules.

Islam See ▷Muslim.

its *and* **it's** **Its** is a possessive adjective. It means 'belonging to it': *Put the parrot back in its cage*. **It's** is a shortened form of 'it is': *It's raining again*.

-ize *or* **-ise** See ▷spelling rules.

jail See ◊gaol.

jargon See ◊clichés, pretentious language, and jargon and ◊plain English.

jejune The word starts like *Jehovah*. The second syllable is stressed, and is pronounced [June].

jetsam See ◊flotsam.

jewellery Spelling: remember the third **e**. US spelling: *jewelry*.

jibe See ◊gibe.

Jocelyn, Joscelin This is now nearly always a female name, but it was originally a male name and is occasionally still given to boys. Either spelling may be used for either sex, but another form, **Joycelin**, is given only to girls.

journey Spelling: remember the **o**.

judgement *or* **judgment** This word can be spelled either way.

judicial *or* **judicious** Judicial pertains to a judge or judgment, as in a court of law, as well as applying more generally to a person or thing that is fair or just: *A special judicial body was set up to determine a fair rent*. **Judicious** is used of good judgement: *The announcer made a judicious pause at this point.*

junta The usual British pronunciation is [jun-ter] to rhyme with *hunter*. It is increasingly common to hear the pronunciation [**hoon**-ter], which sounds like a Northern British pronunciation of *hunter*, and is an approximation to the original Spanish pronunciation. This is the usual US pronunciation.

kaleidoscope Spelling: note the **ei**.

Kenya Nowadays most people say [**Ken**-yer] but before independence people called it [**Keen**-yer], and this pronunciation is still heard.

kerb See ◊curb.

key **Key**, in the sense 'crucial', 'most important', for example *a key issue*, has been overused and has become a cliché. Use it sparingly, if at all.

kilometre The traditional British pronunciation [**kill**-ermeeter] has the advantage that it follows the pattern of *centimetre* and *millimetre*. However, the main US pronunciation [kill-**om**-mitter] appears to be gaining ground in Britain. US spelling: *kilometer*.

kind, sort, *or* **type of** There is a slight difference in meaning and use between *type* and *kind* or *sort*, although they can often be used interchangeably. **Type** is more often found in formal and technical use; it refers to a class, usually small, of things having similar characteristics, belonging to a larger group of related things and with a clear-cut difference from other things or types in the group: *This type of bread is produced without yeast*; *Be sure to use the right cleanser for your skin type*.

    Kind and **sort** are more colloquial and can refer to things or people that are broadly similar, without applying strict criteria. These words should be used with *this, that* rather than *these, those*; phrases such as *I like these kind of books* are often heard but should not be written down. If referring to more than one type, the following noun may be singular or plural: *these types of dog* (or *dogs*). The singular noun is preferable.

    Avoid using *kind, sort,* or *type* unnecessarily; there is no need to say *it's a sort of collie* if the dog is a collie. If it is a particular type of collie, use *type of*. If there is some doubt about the dog's breeding it is better to say *rather like a collie*, or a similar phrase.

kindliness Spelling: the **y** of *kindly* changes to an **i**.

lady *or* **woman** Lady is the feminine equivalent of 'gentleman', and is used as a term of politeness; for example a shop assistant may address a customer as *Madam* and refer to her in her presence as *this lady*, although she may be called *that woman* once she has left the shop. Children are encouraged to refer to an adult female as a *lady* rather than a *woman*, and the female members of a group may be called *the ladies*.

Lady is also used occasionally to describe a woman who is noted for kind and courteous behaviour: *She's a real lady*. In other contexts it sounds a little old-fashioned, and most people now use **woman**. Some women dislike the terms *lady doctor*, *lady teacher*, etc. It is best just to say *doctor* or *teacher* unless there is a good reason to specify the sex; if there is, use *woman*. See also ▷girl.

lamentable The usual pronunciation is with the stress on the first syllable [**lam**-uhn-tble].

languor Spelling: remember the **u**.

last *(Tuesday, etc)* See ▷this (Tuesday, etc).

latter See ▷former.

lawful See ▷legal.

lay *or* **lie** Lay and lie are very easily confused. *Lay* is the present tense of a verb meaning to put something down flat: the past tense is *laid*. *Lay* is also the past tense of the verb *to lie*, meaning to be down flat or to put yourself into that position. The following examples show the tenses of both verbs: *He lays a blanket on the grass and lies down; She laid a blanket on the grass and lay down; They have laid a blanket on the grass and have lain down.*

laziness Spelling: the **y** of *lazy* changes to an **i**.

league Spelling: remember the **u**.

lecherous Spelling: remember there is no **t**.

legal *or* **lawful** If a thing is **legal** it is authorized or permitted by law: *It is perfectly legal to park here*. If it is **lawful** (the word usually precedes a noun) it is done according to the law: *The crowd was asked to disperse in a lawful manner*; *The elder son was the lawful heir to the estate*.

legalese This is a kind of long-winded jargon used by lawyers which it is difficult to understand. Contracts, insurance policies, and guarantees are among the documents in which you may find it. Some businesses and official bodies have had their documents written by ◊Plain English Campaign so that the public can understand them. Others have produced their own plain English documents that have received Plain English Campaign's Crystal Mark for clarity. See also ◊plain English.

lend *or* loan A **loan** is something which is lent, or an act of lending: *I've applied to the bank for a loan*; *We are grateful for the loan of the premises*. In British English, *loan* is used as a verb only when referring formally to a loan of considerable value: *The banks have loaned more than three million pounds to small businesses*; *The Picasso has been loaned to the museum*. In a less formal context, **lend** is used: *Lend me your pen?* In American English the verb *loan* is used for everyday things: *Loan me ten bucks?*.

leopard Spelling: remember the **o**.

Leslie *or* Lesley *Lesley* is the feminine form of the name, *Leslie* the masculine.

letter writing

Letter writing is conventional. There are generally agreed ways of laying out a letter, and people expect to find certain information, such as your address and the date, in certain places. If you do not follow the conventions, you may confuse or irritate the person you are writing to, and generally give a bad impression.

1. Formal personal letters

Opposite is an example of a personal letter of the more formal kind, the sort that you would write not to a relative or friend, but to someone that you know less well.

The first thing to note is the overall **appearance** of a good letter. The page has a space at the top, bottom, and sides, which serves as a frame for the evenly spaced lines of clear writing, typing, or printing. A page that looks like this creates a favourable first impression.

The writer's **address** is in the top righthand corner, with the date underneath it. If you want to add your telephone number, put it on the line below the address or in the top lefthand corner of the page. There are two main ways of laying out the address, the sloping style and the block style.

Tel. 0956 562664   *6 High Street*
                                                          Beeston
                                                          Kent
                                                             CY3 6RB

                                                    25 July 1994

Dear Mr Reynolds,
        Your mother tells me that you have kindly agreed to
talk to the Beeston Preservation Society again. We are most
grateful, and shall look forward to another interesting evening
with more of your beautiful slides.
        The meeting will be in the village hall at 7.30 p.m. I
expect that you will want to arrive a quarter of an hour or so
earlier to get the projector set up and so on
        I will be in touch with you nearer the time to confirm
arrangements.

                            Yours sincerely,
                            Valerie Martin

The sloping style is probably still the more common in Britain, although the block style is gaining ground. In the USA only the block style is used. In the sloping style, start each line of the address a little further to the right than the previous one, so that the lefthand side of the address slopes down from left to right. People who use the sloping style may put a comma at the end of each line of the address except the last, which has a full stop. However, the modern tendency is for no punctuation at all in the address. Letters which have no punctuation in the address often have no comma after *Dear so-and-so* or after the conventional closing phrase before the signature.

In the sloping style, the beginning of the date can continue the lefthand slope of the address, but this makes it difficult to distinguish the date from the address. For this reason, it is preferable to start the date below the beginning of the first line of the address. Some people make it more distinct by leaving a blank line between the address and the date.

The **date** may take various forms. In Britain the most common form is: *6 December 1994*, starting with the number of the day. Endings such as *-th* have rather fallen out of use. Then comes the name of the month in its full form. Finally comes the year in figures. More traditional writers may use a comma to separate the year from the month. In Britain the form with the name of the month first and then the number of the day is also found: *December 6, 1994*. A comma is used to separate the two numbers. This is the only form of the date in the USA.

All-number dates, e.g. 5.7.94., are used only in informal writing. There is a confusing difference between American and British forms, which you need to be aware of in any international situation. For more information see ▷dates. It is always safest to use the name of the month.

In the block style, the beginning of the second line of the address is exactly under the first, and so on. The beginning of the date also lines up with the lefthand side of the address. It is usually separated from the address by a blank line. Here is an example:

> High Street
> Beeston
> Kent
> CY3 6RB
>
> 25 July 1994

After you have written your address and the date, move down and over to the lefthand side. Remember to leave a margin on the left. Then write *Dear So-and-so*.

In formal letters each **paragraph** will deal with a separate aspect of what you have to say. Even in informal letters it helps to put Joe's wedding in one paragraph and your plans for the holiday in another. The most usual way to show that you are starting a paragraph is to *indent* the first line; that is, you start it not at the margin, where the rest of the lines start, but a little further to the right, say about 1.5 cm. Another way to distinguish paragraphs is to leave a blank line between them. This way is often used in typewritten letters.

It is usual to finish a letter with a conventional phrase of goodwill. For people that you know personally but not closely a phrase such as *Best wishes* is suitable. In formal personal letters the standard phrase is *Yours sincerely*. Only the first word in these conventional phrases has a capital letter. Note the spelling of *sincerely*, especially the second *e*. The phrase can be placed in the centre or on the left of the page.

This is also the place for the writer to sign the letter. For family and friends, just the first name is usual. For a person that you know less well, put your first name and surname, or your initials and surname. It is courteous and sensible to write your name clearly. A scrawly signature that no-one can read can make you look self-important or inconsiderate, not at all the effect that you want. There is no full stop after the signature.

For the address on the envelope there is a choice with personal letters between the traditional sloping style and the more modern block style. Use the style that you used in your own address at the head of the letter itself. Start the address about half way down the envelope, leaving a wide margin on the left.

2. Business letters

Tel 4903 988266

23 Seaview Close
Great Yarmouth
Norfolk
NR31 6LT

6 September 1994

The Customer Care Officer
The Traditional Sink Company
Ranworth Road
Norwich
Norfolk
NR1 4KW

Dear Sir/Madam

fireclay sinks

I saw your advertisement for traditional country sinks in August's issue of *Country House*.

I am currently renovating an Edwardian house, and am looking for what I think is known as a gamekeeper's sink, i.e. a large shallow fireclay sink, beige in colour, with a decorative pattern of indentations on the outside.

If you are able to supply such a sink, I should be glad if you would send me details, including the price and the cost of delivery.

Yours faithfully

C. Boswell

Mrs C Boswell

In a letter that you write as a private individual to a company or organization, you put your own **address**, as in a purely personal letter, in the top righthand corner. The block style is common in such letters, and punctuation is often omitted. The date is usually put below the address. There is an example on the previous page.

The most obvious distinguishing feature of the **layout** of a letter to a business is that the name or position and the address of the person that you are writing to appear not only on the envelope but also in the letter itself.

This address is called the *inside address*, and the usual place for it is on the left starting below the level of the date, although it sometimes appears at the bottom of the letter on the left. The inside address (and the address on the envelope) is always in block style, never sloping. In a letter to a business, the date is sometimes written on the left above the inside address.

It is sometimes difficult to know **who to address** in a company. One solution is to put only the name of the company in the inside address, in which case the traditional way of starting the letter is *Dear Sirs*. This has rather an old-fashioned ring now, and is thought sexist by many. You may feel more comfortable writing to someone such as *The Customer Care Officer*, *The Information Officer*, or *The Manager*. In that case you begin the letter *Dear Sir or Madam*. If you know the name of the person you need to write to, use it. Note that *Sir* and *Madam* begin with capital letters. If you start a letter in this way, the conventional ending is *Yours faithfully*. Note that *faithfully* does not have a capital letter. If you know the name of the person you are writing to, you should use it, both in the inside address, and at the beginning of the actual letter. In this case, you should end with *Yours sincerely*.

The traditional polite way of writing a man's name at the top of an address was to put initials or first name and then the surname followed by *Esq*, which was short for *Esquire*, but current practice is to use *Mr* before the name. Note that *Mr* and *Mrs* rarely have a full stop at the end these days, though traditionally minded writers still use them.

When you receive a letter from a business you may find that they have given you a **reference number** for themselves and one for you. If so, they will want you to quote them so that they can trace previous correspondence, or make sure that they keep together all the letters dealing with a particular issue. The usual place to quote references is on the left above the inside address.

It is often helpful to start a letter to a business with a **heading** giving the subject that the letter deals with. For example, if a solicitor is acting for you when you are buying a house, you might write to them about various things that you want them to do in connection with the purchase. You might help them by putting as the first item in your letter:

Purchase of 57 Manor Road, Beccles.

More traditional writers may introduce the subject with the word *re*, pronounced [ree], which comes from Latin, and means 'on the subject of'.

re: purchase of 57 Manor Road, Beccles.

Formal letters from an individual to a company or organization sometimes fall into a regular pattern of **paragraphs**. In the introductory paragraph, you refer to what has prompted you to write. Perhaps you have seen an advertisement for something. Perhaps a product that you bought has proved unsatisfactory. It is sometimes necessary to give detailed information, and this may require more than one paragraph. Then you come to the *purpose* of your letter. This is often to state what action you would like taken. You want the company to send information about a product, for example. Or you want them to replace a faulty item.

In a letter to a business typed on A4 paper it is common not to indent the first line of a paragraph, but to leave a blank line between paragraphs.

In this style of layout it is common to put the final conventional 'signing off' phrase on the left, with the signature underneath it. If you are typing the letter, it is usual to type your name under your signature. A woman may want to give her preferred title here: Miss, Mrs, or Ms. See the example letter. In a handwritten letter she can put it in brackets after her signature.

It is important to be clear about what you want to achieve with your letter, and what points you need to make. Jot them down and put them in order before you start. Forget about 'business English'. Say what you have to say as simply and as briefly as possible. For more detailed advice, see ▷plain English. Your points need to be clear, and they should be expressed courteously. Even when you are complaining, you are more likely to be effective if you are polite.

3. Job applications

One of the most important letters that you ever write may be a letter of application for a job. Even if you are also sending a cv, this letter will give a possible employer their first impression of you. From quite a short letter they will be able to tell a great deal. Are you realistic, well-organized, willing to make an effort to do a good job? Can you concentrate on the job in hand, giving only relevant information? Do you check your facts and your spelling?

If at the first stage you are sending a detailed application form or a cv, the letter will not need to cover all of the same ground, though you could certainly use it to focus attention on recent experience or training that makes you particularly suited to the job. In the USA, where cvs are less commonly demanded, a letter of application needs to cover the details of your educational and professional qualifications, your training and experience that are normally covered in a cv in Britain. For more information on what to include, see ◊curriculum vitae.

liable, apt, likely, *and* **prone** Liable and apt are used before a verb to mean 'having a tendency to': *It's liable to rain in Wales* (it rains quite often); *She's apt to drop in at any time* (you can never tell when she will come). **Prone** is also used in this way, and implies that the tendency is bad: *He's prone to lose his temper with the kids.*

Liable is often used when there is reason to think that something will probably happen in the future, whether or not there is a general tendency for it to do so: *It's liable to rain this afternoon* (because the weather forecast says so and there are black clouds in the sky); *he's liable to lose his temper when he sees what the kids have done* (he does not have much patience with the children, and this particular piece of mischief will probably make him angry).

Likely is also used for things which will probably happen. It can refer to good or bad things, whereas *liable* usually refers to bad: *It's likely to be fine this afternoon*; *No, it's liable to rain.*

Liable and prone are used before a noun to refer to something unwelcome which has a tendency to happen: *The system is liable to error*; *He's prone to fits of temper.* Some people prefer to use *prone* only when referring to a tendency to ill-health: *He's prone to migraines.* However, its use in other contexts is well established, and there is no reason to restrict its use.

liaise Spelling: remember the second **i**.

libel *or* **slander** In English law, **libel** is defamation (the publishing of what is false or derogatory) in permanent form, such as in writing, printing, and radio and TV broadcasts, while **slander** is not in permanent form, so that it is in spoken words or in gestures: *The actor issued a writ for libel*; *Slander is not legally a crime unless it can be proved that special damage was done to the person or persons concerned.*

library Spelling: remember the **rar**.

licence *or* **license** Remember that **licence** is the noun and **license** is the verb. In American English, however, the noun is spelled *license*. To remember the spellings, think of *advice* (noun) and *advise* (verb).

lichen The standard pronunciation is [**lie**-k'n], which corresponds to the word's Greek origin. However, [**lit**-chen], pronounced to rhyme with *kitchen* is also often heard in Britain, and is acceptable.

lie See ◊lay.

lieutenant The British pronunciation is [lef-**ten**-ant] or in the Navy [l'-**ten**-ant], and the US pronunciation [lu-**ten**-ant].

lighted *or* **lit** Either may be used as the past tense and past participle of the verb *to light*. **Lit** is more common.

lightening *or* **lightning** Use **lightening** if you mean 'making lighter', and **lightning** if you mean 'thunder and lightning'.

like *or* **as** **Like** and **as** can both be used before nouns: *It flies like a bird*; *I meant it as a surprise*. The two are not interchangeable: notice the difference between: *Speaking as a father, I deplore these changes* (I am a father, and I speak in that capacity) and: *I want to speak to you like a father* (I am not your father, but I will speak as if I were).

    Like and **as** can also be used before verbs. But whereas *as* is completely acceptable: *She performed the sonata perfectly, as she always does*, *like* is not regarded as part of standard English, and it would not be correct to say: *She performed the sonata perfectly, like she always does*. Similarly, *as if* and *as though* are acceptable: *You look as if you'd seen a ghost*, but *like* should be avoided in formal or careful writing, for example: *You look like you'd seen a ghost*.

    Like and **as** can also be used before adverbs and prepositions. But again, although *as* is completely acceptable: *As with the old model, the new model is fully automated*, *like* is best avoided; it is not correct to say: *Like with the old model, the new model is completely automated*.

likelihood Spelling: note the **i**.

likely See ◊liable.

liquefy Spelling: note the **e** (not an **i**) before the **f**.

liqueur (meaning a sweet alcoholic drink such as fruit liqueurs). The stress is on the second syllable, reflecting the original French pronunciation. The standard British pronunciation is [lick-**cure**]. Spelling: remember **ueu**.

liquor (meaning alcoholic drink in general). It rhymes with *bicker*.
Spelling: remember the **o**.

lit See ◊lighted.

litany See ◊liturgy.

literally This word is often used to emphasize a figurative expression:
My uncle literally died laughing. Correctly used, it shows that an
expression which is usually figurative is to be taken at face value, for
example, if uncle had a fatal heart attack while enjoying a joke.

literature Spelling: note the single **t**, and **a** in the middle (not **i**).

liturgy *or* **litany** A **liturgy** (from the Greek *leitourgia*, 'ministry') is
the form of public services practised by a particular church: *We were
moved by the beauty and solemnity of the Orthodox liturgy.* A **litany**
(from the Late Greek *litaneia*, 'prayer') is a form of prayer consisting of
a series of requests and responses, as well as generally a lengthy list or
recital of something: *Here followeth the LITANY, or General
Supplication* (Book of Common Prayer); *The applicant was faced with a
litany of queries about her work experience.*

livelihood Spelling: note the **i** (not **y**) in the middle.

liveliness Spelling: the **y** of *lively* changes to an **i**.

loan See ◊lend.

loath *or* **loathe** Use **loath** (or **loth**) when you mean reluctant, and
loathe when you mean to hate.

locale See ◊location.

locality See ◊location.

locate **Located** means 'situated': *The shop was located next to the
cinema.* **Locate** can be used to mean 'find' if it refers to a particular
thing which stays in the same place: *We located the shop: it was next to
the cinema.* It should not be used in this sense for a person or a movable
thing, or for an example of the kind of thing sought, rather than the
actual one: *We did not find the shop we were looking for, but we found*
(**not** located) *one next to the cinema.*

location, locality, *or* **locale** A **location** is the place where
something is situated: *The new flats were built in a pleasant riverside
location.* A **locality** is similar, but unless qualified (*exact locality*) has a
wider sense: *Our hotel was in an attractive locality not far from the sea.*

A **locale** is a place linked to a particular event or series of events: *The director found an ideal locale for his new film.*

loneliness Spelling: the **y** of *lonely* changes to an **i**.

longevity The main stress is on the second syllable, and the **g** is soft as in *jam*. The pronunciation is [lon-**jev**-ity].

longitude Spelling: note that there is no **t** after the **g**.

loveliness Spelling: the **y** of *lovely* changes to an **i**.

lower case See ▷case, upper and lower.

luxurious *or* **luxuriant** **Luxurious** is used of something that has or gives luxury: *The house was expensively furnished, with luxurious carpeting throughout.* **Luxuriant** is used of something rich and abundant: *Joanna slowly brushed her long, luxuriant hair; We were awed by the luxuriant ornamentation of the Buddhist temples.*

machination The standard pronunciation is [mackin-**ay**-shun], the stressed syllable rhyming with *day*. The pronunciation [mashin-**ay**-shun] is also heard.

macho The first syllable is stressed and is pronounced [match].

macrocosm See ◊microcosm.

magic *or* **magical** **Magic** relates to magic: *Dreams are like magic spells: we are held captive and have no power to escape.* **Magical** relates to something that seems like magic: *It was a magical moment: the whole coast was suddenly bathed in the rays of the setting sun.*

maintenance Spelling: remember the **e**.

major The primary meaning of **major** is 'the greater or more important of two things'. It is often used to mean 'very important' or 'most significant'. This is not incorrect, but *major* is rather overused in this sense. It can be replaced by such words as *important, principal, foremost, main, serious, grave*, or their synonyms.

majority, minority These refer to a greater or lesser number, and should not be used with a single entity: *The majority of people fritter their money away*, not *The majority of the money is frittered away*. The exception is in cases like *a minority of the committee*, which actually means a minority of the members of the committee. Many people find it difficult to decide whether to use a singular or plural verb with words like *majority*. The word itself is singular, but *the majority of people is* looks odd because the singular verb comes immediately after the plural noun.

In British English, a plural verb is used if the real subject of the sentence is *the people*: *The majority of people agree with the government*. If the subject is *the majority*, a singular verb is used: *The government's majority has grown*. This also applies to terms like *a lot of, a number of*, which are technically singular: *A lot of children no longer have school dinners*; *The number of children having school dinners has shrunk* (the number has shrunk, the children may well have grown).

A quick test to find the real subject is to try substituting *many* or *most* for *majority, a number of,* and *fewer* for *minority* etc. If the sentence still makes sense a plural verb is needed. This applies even if the real subject of the sentence is not stated but understood: *The majority agree with the government*; *A lot no longer have school dinners*.

malign The stress is on the second syllable, and the word is pronounced [m'**line**]. Spelling: remember the **g**.

man, mankind The word **man** has always had two meanings, 'human being' and 'adult male', but a few people feel that the use of *man* in the word *mankind* and phrases such as *Stone Age man* excludes women. In these cases the meaning is clearly 'humans', and most people have no qualms about using *man* or *mankind*. For those that do, or if it is important to emphasize that both men and women are referred to, the following may be suitable in some contexts: *men and women, people, persons, the population, the community, everyone, folk, mortals, humans, human beings, the human race. Personkind* exists, but is not recommended as it sounds unnatural, either contrived or facetious.

manageable Spelling: remember to leave the **e** in.

mandatory The standard pronunciation is with the stress on the first syllable [**man**-der-tree], but a pronunciation with the stress on the second syllable is also heard [man-**day**-ter-ree]. The US pronunciation has the stress on the first syllable [**man**-der-tory].

mannequin *or* **manikin** Both words are now rather old-fashioned, but as applied to people a **mannequin** is a (female) fashion model and a **manikin** is a (male) dwarf: *Mannequin parades were a regular feature of the fashion world in the 1930s*; *The children loved the story about the giant and the manikin.*

manœuvre The stress is on the second syllable, and the word is pronounced [m'**noo**-vuh]. Spelling: note the **œu**. US spelling: *maneuver*.

mantle *or* **mantel** Use **mantle** when you mean a cloak, or something that covers like a cloak. Use **mantel** when you mean a shelf over a fireplace, now better known as a mantelpiece.

margarine Most British people say [marge-er-**reen**] with a soft **g** with the sound of **j** in *jam*. A few people, mostly older, use a hard **g** like the one in *go* and think that the soft **g** is not really correct. The standard US pronunciation has the stress on the first syllable and then two weak syllables [**marge**-er-reen].

marital *or* **matrimonial** Both words refer to marriage. **Marital** is more personal, relating to the husband or the wife (or to both husband and wife): *The couple began to experience marital problems*, (differences between husband and wife); *They looked forward to a long life of marital happiness*. **Matrimonial** is more impersonal, relating to marriage as a state: *They began to experience matrimonial problems* (something went wrong with the marriage).

maroon Spelling: remember one **r**.

marquis *or* **marquess** The title is normally spelt **marquis** for a foreign nobleman (next in rank above a count) and **marquess** for a British nobleman (next in rank above an earl but below a duke): *The Marquis de Sade, who gave his name to sadism, was not really a marquis at all but a French count; The Marquess of Bath opened Britain's first safari park at Longleat in 1967.*

mastectomy Spelling: remember the first **t**.

masterly *or* **masterful** Something **masterly** is clever or skilful, as befits a master: *The batsman then played a masterly stroke which ensured the victory of the side*. A person or thing that is **masterful** is imperious or commanding, befitting one who is master: *She is a proud and masterful woman, and intimidating on first acquaintance*.

matrimonial See ▷marital.

mattress Spelling: remember the double **t**.

may *or* **might** **May** and **might** both express the idea of possibility: *We may go to Rhodes next year; We might go to Rhodes next year*. To a large extent these overlap in meaning, but the smaller the possibility, the more appropriate it is to use *might*: *We might go to Rhodes next year, although my wife's not too keen.*

   May and **might** can both refer to present and future possibilities: *They may/might prefer to stay here*. But only *might* can be used with reference to the past: *She said they might go to Rhodes next year.*

   In standard English, *may have* and *might have* have different meanings. **May have** means that you don't yet know whether something has happened – the possibility is still open: *There's been no news of the climbers, and there are fears that they may have been killed*. **Might have** means that there was a possibility of something but that it no longer exists: *You were lucky the gun didn't go off – you might have been killed.*

   There is an increasing tendency to use *may have* in place of *might have*: *You were lucky the gun didn't go off- you may have been killed*. In most cases the meaning will be perfectly clear from the context, but occasionally ambiguity may arise, and the *may have/might have* distinction is a useful one to keep.

See also ▷can or may.

media Media is the plural of *medium*, in the sense 'a means of mass communication'. **The media** can be used to refer to these means collectively (i.e. radio, television, newspapers, etc taken together), but it should still be followed by a plural verb: *The media are full of scandal.* Avoid using *media* to refer to one means of communication (a *medium*): do not say, *the headlines in the media*, if you mean just the newspapers.

Note that the plural of *medium* in other senses can be *media* or *mediums*; in the sense 'a person who attempts to communicate with the dead' the plural is *mediums*.

medicine The standard pronunciation has two syllables [**med**-suhn], with the stress on the first syllable and a weak second syllable, but there are several acceptable variations including [**med**-sin] and [**med**-iss-sin]. Spelling: remember **i** after the **d**, not **e**.

Mediterranean Spelling: remember one **t** and two **rs**.

metallurgy The standard British pronunciation is with the stress on the second syllable, which rhymes with *pal*. The end is like the end of *biology*. Another accepted pronunciation has the stress on the first syllable. The first two syllables sound the same as *metal*. The US pronunciation also begins with [metal] and the **r** is pronounced.

metre *or* **meter** In their most obvious applications, a **metre** is a measure (just over three feet) and a **meter** a measuring device: *The gas meter is about a metre from the back door.* This means that words ending in -*metre* relate to a length and those in -*meter* apply to a measuring instrument: *The speedometer showed how fast we were travelling in kilometres per hour.* However, the US spelling of all -*metre* words is meter: *Like the British, Americans reckon distances in miles, not kilometers.*

metric *or* **metrical** Metric is to do with the metre (see above) that is the unit of length, while **metrical** relates to the metre that is found in verse: *Britain converted its currency to the metric system in 1971; A hexameter is a line of verse with six metrical feet.*

microcosm *or* **macrocosm** A microcosm is something that represents the universe, or humanity, in miniature: *A single human being* *is a microcosm of the whole of humanity; Their village was a microcosm of our world.* A **macrocosm** is essentially the converse, and is a term either for the universe or for any complete structure that contains smaller structures: *Society is the macrocosm of each of its individual members.*

might See ◊may.

mightiness Spelling: the **y** of *mighty* changes to an **i**.

migraine [**Mee**-grain] is probably the main British pronunciation, but [**my**-grain] is also widespread. In the USA the standard pronunciation is [**my**-grain].

mileage *or* **milage** This word can be spelled either way.

militate See ◊mitigate.

millennium Spelling: remember double **l** and double **n**.

millepede *or* **millipede** This word can be spelled either way.

mineralogy Spelling: note the **a** before the **l**, not **o**.

miniature Spelling: remember the **a**.

minority See ◊majority.

minuscule Spelling: note the **u** before the **s**, not **i**.

minute Spelling: note the **u**.

mischievous Spelling: remember there is no **i** after the **v**.

misspell Note that this word has two **ss** (*mis-* plus *-spell*).

mistrust See ◊distrust.

misuse See ◊abuse.

mitigate *or* **militate** To **mitigate** something is to moderate it or make it less severe: *The offence was mitigated by the fact that the offender had not seen the warning notice.* To **militate** against something is to affect or influence it adversely: *The bad weather militated against the planned outing.* People sometimes say *mitigate against* instead of *militate against* but this is incorrect and should be avoided.

moat See ◊mote.

moccasin Spelling: note the two **cs** and one **s**.

modal verb A verb that, when used with other verbs, expresses such things as certainty, possibility, wishes, or intentions. The main modal verbs are: *may/might; will/would; can/could; shall/should; must.*

Mohammedan See ◊Muslim.

mollusc US spelling: *mollusk*.

mortgage Spelling: remember the **t**.

Moslem See ◊Muslim.

mote This word (meaning 'speck') should not be confused with *moat*, meaning 'a ditch round a castle'.

mould US spelling: *mold*.

moult US spelling: *molt*.

moustache US spelling: *mustache*.

Ms This came into use in the early 1970s, when it was adopted by feminists who did not wish to be publicly labelled as married or single, and some people still use it, or disapprove of it, for this reason. Nowadays it is often used to refer to women whose marital status is not known, and most people find this acceptable and useful. A woman should be addressed by the form she uses herself, whatever your own feelings on the subject. This is not to make a stand for or against feminism; it is simply good manners.

mucous *or* **mucus** Remember that **mucous** is the adjective and **mucus** is the noun.

murkiness Spelling: the **y** of *murky* changes to an **i**.

muscle (meaning the parts of the body used for movement). Do not confuse this with *mussel*, the shellfish. Spelling: remember the **c**.

Muslim *Muslim*, not *Moslem*, is the preferred spelling. *Mohammedan* is old-fashioned and disliked by Muslims. The religion is called *Islam*, with the adjective *Islamic*: *Islamic art*. *Muslim* refers to the followers of Islam: *the British Muslim community*.

mussel See ◊muscle.

mutual *or* **common** Mutual refers to a feeling that two or more people or groups have towards each other: *the mutual love between husband and wife*; *We do not trust them, and the feeling is mutual*; or to something that two or more people or groups do to or for each other: *Nuclear war can only result in mutual destruction*; *a self-help group for mutual support*. *Mutual* is also often used to refer to a feeling, interest, etc that two people have about a third person or thing: *a mutual love of sailing*. Some people consider this to be incorrect, and would use *common* instead. Applied to people, *mutual* is more or less accepted, as *common* might suggest inferiority: *We met through a mutual friend*.

Avoid using *mutual* if the idea is expressed elsewhere in the sentence, for example by *cooperate*, *each other* or *share*: *We shared a love of sailing*.

myself Myself is the first person singular reflexive pronoun: *I cut myself shaving*. Linked to a noun by *and* or another conjunction, it can be used as the subject of a sentence: *My husband and myself are pleased to accept your invitation*; and as an ordinary, non-reflexive object of a verb or preposition: *This is a great honour for Trevor and myself*.

This strikes many people as an excessively genteel usage (perhaps arising out of uncertainty over whether to use 'I' or 'me' in ▷compound subjects). It is more straightforward to use 'I' as a subject: *My husband and I are pleased to accept your invitation*, and 'me' as an object: *This is a great honour for Trevor and me*.

mysterious, mystic, *or* **mystical** Mysterious relates to something difficult to explain and possibly also awesome in an 'otherworldly' sense: *There was a mysterious silence there in the wood*; *Several people reported seeing mysterious lights in the sky*.

Mystic is somewhat similar, but emphasizes the supernatural or spiritual factor: *We heard of mystic rites and ceremonies*; *Miranda had a mystic beauty that long haunted me*. **Mystical** is the same as *mystic* but relates solely to what is spiritual: *Trees had a mystical power for the Druids*.

mythical *or* **mythological** In its general sense, **mythical** relates to anything imaginary, while both *mythical* and **mythological** refer to mythology, and especially to the myths of classical times: *What happened to that mythical fortune of his?; Her favourite mythological character in Greek legend was Ganymede*.

naive *or* **naïve** This word can be spelled either way.

nastiness Spelling: the **y** of *nasty* changes to an **i**.

naturalist *or* **naturist** A **naturalist** is a person who is interested in botany or zoology: *Sheila is an enthusiastic naturalist, and has a particular interest in woodland life.* A **naturist** is a nudist: *A section of the sea front at Brighton is reserved for naturists.*

naught *or* **nought** Naught means 'nothing' in certain idiomatic expressions: *All his plans came to naught when the firm went bankrupt.* **Nought** is the figure '0' (zero): *How many noughts are there in a million?; Let's play noughts and crosses.* Bear this distinction in mind when spelling these two words. In American English, however, the spelling *naught* is used for both senses.

naughtiness Spelling: the **y** of *naughty* changes to an **i**.

naval *or* **navel** The words are unrelated in origin and meaning. **Naval** is to do with the navy; the **navel** is the umbilicus ('tummy button'): *He was dressed as a naval officer*; *A navel orange has a small pit like a navel in the top.*

necessary Spelling: remember one **c** and two **ss**.

Negro See ▷black.

neither Spelling: note the **ei**.
In standard English, **neither** on its own is used with a singular verb: *Do not attempt to bring livestock or plant material into the country; neither is permitted.* But in colloquial English, it is completely acceptable to use a plural verb: *Neither are permitted.* Similarly when *neither* is followed by *of*, it is common to use a plural verb: *Neither of her parents are alive*, but a singular verb is more appropriate for formal writing: *Neither of her parents is alive.*

   When it is followed by *nor*, the verb agrees with the noun or pronoun that comes after the *nor*. If this is singular, the verb is singular: *Neither I nor your father was told about it.* But if it is plural, the verb is plural: *Neither the French nor the Italians have qualified for the finals.*

If one noun or pronoun refers to a male person and the other to a female person, it is permissible to use a plural verb and plural pronouns, in order to avoid the invidious 'he': *Neither Beth nor Tim have collected their tickets*.

When you use **neither ... nor**, it is preferable to put both the *neither* and the *nor* immediately in front of the parts of the sentence they refer to. *She will eat neither meat nor dairy products* is more acceptable than: *She will neither eat meat nor dairy products*.

When *neither* is a pronoun, it refers only to two things or people. For three or more things or people, use *none*. But when it is a conjunction, it is perfectly acceptable to use it for three or more things or people: *The prisoners were allowed neither food, sleep nor washing facilities for 48 hours*.

nephew See ◊cousin.

next *(Tuesday, etc)* See ◊this (Tuesday, etc).

nice Used of people, *nice* means 'pleasant', 'affable' (except of young women, where it also means 'conventionally well-behaved'). In other contexts *nice* has been so overused as a vague term of approval that it has become almost meaningless.

It is often better to be more specific: *a delicious meal*; *a comfortable (cosy, spacious, beautiful) house*; *a pretty (funny, appropriate) birthday card*.

Sometimes, however, the vagueness of *nice* is useful: *that's a nice hat* is all that is needed to pay a compliment, and a more specific word might reveal that your opinion of the hat's good points is not the same as the wearer's.

niche There are two common British pronunciations, [neesh] and [nitch], the first perhaps being more highly regarded. The US pronunciation is always [nitch].

niece See ◊cousin.

noisiness Spelling: the **y** of *noisy* changes to an **i**.

nominative case The case of a noun or pronoun that is the subject of a sentence. All pronouns have a nominative form: *I, you, we, she, they*, for example. Most pronouns have a different form when they are in the accusative case, that is, when they are objects: *me, us, her, him*.

none *None is* or *none are*? When *none* refers to a singular noun, the answer is easy – *is*: *I needed money immediately, but none was available; None of this meat is worth keeping*.

But when *none* refers to a plural noun, doubts can arise. This is because the fallacious idea has been implanted in the minds of English speakers that *none* means 'not one' and therefore, like *one*, must have a singular verb. It conflicts with the natural tendency of the English language, which is to make the verb agree with the noun to which the pronoun refers – if the noun is plural, then the verb is plural.

The result is that in a plural context, both a plural verb: *None of my friends were there* and a singular verb: *None of my friends was there* can be used. In general, a plural verb sounds more natural and unaffected, and is to be preferred. It has the particular advantage that an accompanying plural pronoun avoids the sexist 'he' or 'she' and the ponderous 'he or she' in cases where the sex of the referent is unknown or unspecified: *None of the directors of the company stand to lose their own money*. And sometimes it would simply be ridiculous to insist on the singular – for instance, where *none* is used in specific comparison with a plural noun: *None of our dancers are as talented as the Russians*.

non-flammable See ▷inflammable.

nonwhite See ▷black.

not The position of **not** within a sentence can substantially affect the meaning of the sentence.

Not all and *not every* imply 'some': *Not all his novels were bestsellers* (but some of them were). If *not* comes after *all* or *every*, it can have the same meaning, but it is also open to the interpretation 'none': *All his novels were not bestsellers* (but some of them were *or* none of them were). When you speak, you can make clear which you mean by the way you say it, but in writing that is not possible, so if there is any danger of real ambiguity, it is best to recast the sentence.

Not can also present problems when it is used with *because*. Does *We didn't appoint him because of his age* mean that his age was not the reason why we appointed him, or that because he was too young or too old we didn't appoint him? If there is a genuine possibility that both interpretations could be made, it is better to rewrite the sentence in an unambiguous form.

noticeable Spelling: remember to keep the **e**.

nought See ▷naught.

noun This is a grammatical part of speech that names a person, animal, object, quality, idea, or time. In English many simple words are both noun and verb: *jump; reign; rain*. Adjectives are sometimes used as nouns: *a local man; one of the locals*.

A **common noun** does not begin with a capital letter: *child; cat*, whereas a **proper noun** does, because it is the name of a particular person, animal, or place: *Jane; Rover; Norfolk*. A **concrete noun** refers to things that can be sensed: *dog; box*, whereas an **abstract noun** relates to generalizations abstracted from life as we observe it: *fear; condition; truth*. A **countable noun** can have a plural form: *book: books*, while an **uncountable noun** or mass noun cannot: *dough; weather*. Many English nouns can be used both countably and uncountably, for example, *wine: Have some wine; it's one of our best wines*.

A **collective noun** is singular in form but refers to a group: *flock; family; committee*, and a **compound noun** is made up of two or more nouns: *teapot; baseball team; car-factory; strike committee*. A **verbal noun** is formed from a verb as a gerund or otherwise: *build: building; regulate: regulation*.

number Number is a feature of nouns, verbs and pronouns. In present-day English it consists of two categories: **singular** and **plural**. Singular nouns and pronouns: *car; I; it* generally take a singular verb, plural nouns and pronouns: *cars; we; they* generally take a plural verb.

In practice there is little difference between singular and plural in English verbs. In the past tense they are identical. In the present tense, the only difference is that the third person singular usually has an **s** on the end, whereas the plural and the first and second person singular do not: *I come, he comes, they come*. Exceptions to this are the modal or auxiliary verbs, such as: *can, may, will*, which do not have an **s** in the third person singular *she can*; and the verb *to be*, which has distinctive forms in the first and third person singular in both the present and the past tenses.

Some singular nouns which refer to groups of people or animals can take a plural verb. To find out more about this, see ▷collective noun.

It can often happen that another noun or pronoun comes between the verb and its grammatical subject. If this is different in number from the subject, it can affect the number of the verb: *The contents of the book submitted to our legal department has raised a few eyebrows*. The subject of the verb here is *contents*, not *book* or *department*, so the verb should be plural: *have*, not singular: *has*.

Nouns and pronouns linked by *and* can take a plural or a singular verb. To find out more about this, see ▷compound subject.

Measurements of quantity, distance, etc, that contain a plural noun can be regarded as a single unit, and therefore take a singular verb: *Fifty pounds is too much to pay*; *Twenty miles is a long way to walk*.

There are some nouns ending in **-s** that take a singular verb: *The news is good*. They include the names of certain games: *Darts is my favourite game* and the names of certain diseases: *Mumps is unpleasant for adult males to catch*. Some nouns ending in **-s** take a singular verb when they denote an area of study: *Acoustics is a tricky subject* but a plural verb when they have another meaning: *The acoustics of the hall aren't very good*.

numerous, numerable, *or* **innumerable** Numerous means 'great in number': *He rang on numerous occasions* (several times). **Numerable** is used of something that can be numbered or counted: *There were so many islands that they were scarcely numerable*. **Innumerable** means 'countless', and is stronger in sense than *numerous*: *He rang on innumerable occasions* (very many times).

obelisk Spelling: remember the **e**.

object The noun or other word that is the recipient of the action of the verb in a sentence.

obscene Spelling: remember the **sc**.

observant Spelling: remember the ending **-ant**, not **-ent**.

observatory Spelling: remember the **o** after the **t**.

occasion Spelling: note the double **c** and only one **s**.

occupy Spelling: note the double **c**.

occurrence Spelling: note the double **c** and double **r** (although *occur* has a single **r**).

odorous Spelling: note there is no **u** before the **r**, unlike *odour*.

offence US spelling: *offense*.

official *or* **officious** Official relates to someone or something formal or authoritative: *Here is an official announcement; Arthur Smith was there in his official capacity as chairman.* **Officious** is used of a person who is unnecessarily keen to offer advice or services, often intrusively or embarrassingly so: *Guests were greeted by an officious little man who made it his business to take their coats.*

officialese This is a kind of jargon used in government offices, which is difficult for the public to understand. Forms and standard letters are among the documents in which you may find it. Certain government departments have reformed. Some have had their documents written by Plain English Campaign. Others have produced their own plain English documents, which have been granted Plain English Campaign's Crystal Mark for clarity. See also ▷plain English.

officious See ▷official.

often The standard pronunciation is [**off**-n]. Some people pronounce the **t**. There is an upper class pronunciation [**orf**-n], and this is also the standard US pronunciation.

older See ◊elder.

omelette Spelling: remember the double **t**. US spelling: *omelet*.

omitted Spelling: note the single **m**.

on behalf of See ◊behalf.

on the part of See ◊behalf.

on to *or* **onto** Some people consider **on to** to be correct, although **onto** is now widely used and accepted. It is sometimes useful in avoiding ambiguity: *He walked on to the common* (he walked on until he reached the common), but: *He walked onto the common* (he reached the common and began to walk on it).

one *or* **you** One, meaning 'anybody', is now thought of as rather formal and old-fashioned. **You** is acceptable except in very formal contexts, although you may sometimes need to make it clear that the person you are speaking to should not take what you say personally. Whichever you use, be consistent: *one should go oneself* or *you should go yourself*, not *one should go yourself*. Do not use *one* to mean 'I': Oscar Wilde's statement, *'I do not mind waiting in the carriage... provided there is somebody to look at one'* was meant to sound pompous and conceited, but *one* used in this way usually does, whatever the speaker's intention.

one of The singular phrase **one of** is usually followed by a plural noun or pronoun. This can sow a seed of doubt in people's minds about the verb that comes afterwards – should it be singular or plural? The answer depends on whether the verb goes with *one* or with the plural noun or pronoun: *One of my old school friends is coming to stay next week*. In this sentence, it is only one of the school friends that is coming to stay. *One* is the subject of the verb, so the verb is singular – *is*.

It's one of those books that keep you gripped until the very end*. In this sentence, it is all the books that keep you gripped, not just this one. *Those books is the subject of the verb, so the verb is plural – keep*.

The noun or pronoun following **one of** is usually plural (if it is not plural, then it is a collective singular, like *group* or *gang*). But putting in an extra phrase can disrupt the link between *one of* and its noun or pronoun, as in this sentence: *'In England the main object seems to be what is after all one of the most, if not **the** most, important gastronomic principle...'*. The singular *principle* is incorrect, and sounds very odd, but it would have sounded equally odd to use the plural *principles*. The best solution in such cases is to rewrite the sentence: *one of the most important gastronomic principles, if not **the** most important.*

only The natural place in a sentence for **only**, as for most adverbs, is next to the verb. Its meaning may stretch out to affect other words, but when you speak you can make this clear by the way you say the sentence. There is no need to move *only*.

However, when you write, that option is closed off, and ambiguity can creep in. For example, does a sign in a station saying: *This platform only for Olympia* mean that trains from this platform go to Olympia and to nowhere else, or that trains do not go to Olympia from any platform other than this one?

If there is a danger of misunderstanding, it is best either to put *only* next to the word it relates to: *Only I* (I and no one else) *saw the accident*; *I only saw* (did not hear, etc) *the accident*; *I saw only the accident* (I did not see anything else); or, if the result is inappropriately formal for its context, to recast the sentence without *only*: *I and no one else saw the accident*.

openness Spelling: note the double **n**.

ophthalmic Spelling: remember the **ph**.

opossum Spelling: note the single **p** and double **s**.

opponent Spelling: remember the double **p**.

opportunity Spelling: note the double **p**, and the **or**.

oppress Spelling: remember the double **p**.

oral See ◊aural.

ordinance *or* **ordnance** Remember that **ordinance** means a regulation or decree, whereas **ordnance** means military equipment or weapons. It is also used in Ordnance Survey maps, which were originally produced by the artillery department.

ordinarily The standard British pronunciation has the stress on the first syllable, then two weak syllables before the final one [**ord**-n-ruh-lee]. Some people put the stress on the third syllable [ord-n-**air**-ruh-lee], but many people disapprove of this pronunciation. The US pronunciation is similar, [ord-n-**e**-ruh-lee].

ordnance See ◊ordinance.

orient *and* **orientate** Both originally meant 'to face, *or* to make something face, the east'. Both are now used to mean 'get one's bearings', 'adjust to a new situation'. **Orient** is preferred in American English and in technical use; in everyday British English there is no preference.

oscillate Spelling: remember the **sc** and the double **l**.

outspokenness Spelling: remember the double **n**.

overrated Spelling: remember the double **r**.

overreact Spelling: remember the double **r**.

override Spelling: remember the double **r**.

overrule Spelling: remember the double **r**.

overrun Spelling: remember the double **r**.

owing to See ▷due to.

pageant Spelling: note the **ea**.

palate *or* **palette** The **palate** is literally the roof of the mouth, and so the means of testing the taste of something, or the pleasure of taste itself: *Too much junk food can ruin your palate*; *The white wine appealed to her palate*. A **palette** is the board on which an artist mixes paints to make different colours. It is sometimes used to refer to a range of colours.

pallor Spelling: note there is no **u** after the **o**.

panacea A **panacea** is a remedy for all diseases or problems. There is no need to use *all* after it: *a panacea for our economic problems* means a remedy that will solve all the problems of the economy. It is sometimes misused to mean a remedy which is extremely effective for a specific problem: *a panacea for the common cold*. Avoid this.

panache Spelling: note the **ch**.

paprika British English has two pronunciations, [**pap**-rica] with an ending like the ending of *Africa*, and [per-**preek**-ker], which is also the US pronunciation.

paradigm The beginning is pronounced the same as the beginning of *paratrooper*, and the end is pronounced [dime].

paraffin Spelling: note the single **r** and two **f**s.

paragraph A paragraph is a section of a piece of writing, and deals with ONE aspect of the subject dealt with in the whole.

One sentence in the paragraph, the so-called *topic sentence*, should make clear what this aspect is. It is typically the first sentence. All the other sentences in the paragraph should relate clearly and logically to the topic announced in this sentence, and develop it in some way. They may do this by going into detail, by illustrating it with examples, by supporting the idea in it with evidence, by comparison or contrast or analogy, most often by a combination of these methods.

The connection of one sentence to another should be logical, and can be made clearer to the reader by special words and phrases. Here are

some examples:
– adding another point in an argument: *The concerts are quite unsuitable for young children. They are long.* **Besides**, *they are late at night.*
– contrasting one idea with another: *Austria has produced leading theorists of the free market economy.* **However**, *it has a larger state-controlled sector than any other western nation.*
– giving an example: *Vegetables were cheaper. Carrots,* **for example**, *were only 15p a pound.*
– summing up: *His qualifications are not appropriate. He has never worked with children before, and does not seem aware of the responsibilities involved.* **In short**, *he is unsuitable for the post.*
– spelling out an implication: *Young people do not have enough money for them, and older people do not choose to buy them.* **In other words**, *there is no market for them.*
– showing a result: *He can no longer obtain good quality materials.* **For this reason**, *he has been forced to move towards the lower end of the market.*
– making clear the order of events: *She was sentenced to fifteen years' imprisonment, and died before her release. It* **subsequently** *became clear that she was innocent.*

As well as making clear the relations between sentences, you need to make clear the relations between paragraphs.

The following is an example of a well-constructed paragraph. The numbers inserted into the text relate to the comments below it.

(1) From this children's charter of 1833 came (2) the Ten Hours Bill, (3) which limited the work of women and youths in textile factories to ten hours a day. (4) Consequently, men too could no longer work more than ten hours a day, (5) for they were unable to keep the factory processes going without the women and youths. (6) This limitation of working hours had been for years the goal of the employees, and a subject of great controversy. (7) It laid the foundation for the mass of legislation which now governs conditions and hours in all branches of industry.

(1) link to previous paragraph
(2) announcement of the topic of this paragraph: the Ten Hours Bill
(3) development by definition
(4) showing result
(5) showing the reason for the result
(6) and (7) showing the significance of the bill

The first sentence makes very clear what the topic is. The unity of the paragraph can be seen in the ease with which one can give it a title, *the Ten Hours Bill*, and in the fact that every sentence is relevant when tested against that title.

parallelogram Spelling: note the double **l** then single **l**.

parameter In general use, **parameter** refers to a distinguishing characteristic or factor, especially one that can be measured or quantified: *the parameters of light are brightness and colour*. It has come to be used loosely to mean a limit. This is not incorrect, but it sounds like jargon. Before using it consider whether *limit; scope; boundary,* or a similar word would be more suitable.

parenthesis The practice in written or printed language of placing certain statements between a pair of such punctuation marks as commas, dashes, and brackets, to show that they are asides or interruptions in the normal flow of text.

parliament Spelling: remember the **i**.

part, on the part of, on someone's part See ◊behalf.

participles English verbs have two types of participle: the present participle and the past participle. The **present participle** ends in *-ing*. It is used in forming the continuous or progressive tenses of a verb: *He's sleeping*; *She was combing her hair*. Many present participles can be used as adjectives: *a sleeping baby*. Some such adjectives can be used as plural nouns: *the living and the dead*. The present participle can also be used as a noun denoting the action of a verb (see ◊gerund) and as a noun denoting a result of the action of the verb: *She showed me her paintings*.

The **past participle** usually ends in *-ed*, although some verbs have special past participial forms e.g. *chosen; gone; slept; swum*. It is used in forming the perfect tenses of a verb: *They've disappeared*; *I hadn't meant to do it*. It is also used to form the passive: *He can't be blamed for it*. Many past participles can be used as adjectives: *I was surprised to hear the news*; *She had a surprised look on her face*. Some such adjectives can be used as nouns: *Advise the accused of his rights*.

passive The form of a verb, using *to be*, where the subject of the sentence is affected by the action rather than performing it: *James was surprised by the news*, rather than: *The news surprised James*. See also ◊active.

past *or* passed Past is never a verb: *The time for pleasure is past* (adjective); *We ate there several times in the past* (noun); *It's half past* *seven already* (preposition); *Sandra hurried past* (adverb). **Passed** is always a verb: *Sandra passed in a hurry*; *Many of the students had already passed the exam.*

patent The usual British pronunciation for all senses of this word is [**pay**-tuhnt]. In technical usage, when it refers to the legal protection of an invention, the word is often pronounced [**pat**-uhnt]. Americans use [**pat**-uhnt] for all uses of the word except 'obvious', for which they use [**pay**-tuhnt].

pathetic This means 'giving rise to pity': *pathetic television pictures of starving children*; *a pathetic attempt to hold on to the life-raft*. It is also widely used to mean 'very bad', 'inadequate', 'deserving contempt or scorn': *What a pathetic excuse!*. Avoid this in formal contexts.

patisserie Spelling: note the one **t** and two **ss**.

pavilion Spelling: note the single **l**.

peaceful *or* **peaceable** Peaceful is to do with a state of peace or calm: *The park was a peaceful scene, with children playing and pensioners strolling*. **Peaceable** is to do with wanting or seeking peace: *The deer is a peaceable animal*; *We reached a peaceable settlement.*

pedal *or* **peddle** To **pedal** is to move by pedalling, as on a bicycle:*The children pedalled down the road*. To **peddle** is to sell things from door to door: *The salesman was peddling his wares wherever he could*. The words are not related.

pejorative The standard British pronunciation is [pidge-**orr**-ertive], the middle part rhyming with *horror*. Some traditionalists put the stress on the first syllable, and say [**peej**-er-uhtive]. The US pronunciation is [pidge-**jaw**-ruhtive].

pendant (meaning necklace). Remember the **-ant** and do not confuse it with *pendent* (an adjective meaning 'hanging').

penicillin Spelling: remember the single **n** and double **l**.

peninsula *or* **peninsular** Peninsula is the noun and **peninsular** the adjective.

penniless Spelling: note the **i**, not **y**.

per cent *or* **percentage point** When the Chancellor announces that he has reduced the bank rate by one **per cent**, he usually means that he has reduced it by one *percentage point*. If the bank rate was ten per cent, a fall of one per cent would be a fall of one per cent (one hundredth) of ten per cent, and the new bank rate would be 9.99%.

A **percentage point** is a unit expressing the difference between two percentages; a fall of one percentage point would be a fall from ten to nine per cent. In American English *per cent* is spelt as one word, *percent*.

perceptive, percipient, perspicacious, *or* **perspicuous** A **perceptive** person understands something readily or intuitively: *So you realized I had lost? That was very perceptive of you.* A **percipient** person is similar, but notices whatever it is quickly: *The youngest members of the class were often the most percipient.*

A **perspicacious** person is one who discerns or who understands something without needing an explanation: *He was a perspicacious student of human nature, and knew how we would react.* A **perspicuous** person is easy to understand: *We then heard Anna's account, which although long was wonderfully clear and perspicuous.*

percipient See ◊perceptive.

perennial Spelling: remember the single **r** and double **n**.

permanent Spelling: note the ending **-ent**.

person Person is a feature of verbs and pronouns. It consists of three categories: **first person**, which denotes the speaker; **second person**, which denotes the person spoken to; and **third person**, which denotes the person or thing spoken about.

The first-person pronouns are *I* and *we*; the second-person pronoun is *you*; and the third-person pronouns are *he, she, it* and *they*.

I and *we* take first-person verb forms; *you* takes second-person verb forms; and nouns and *he, she, it* and *they* take third-person verb forms. In the past tense all these verb forms are identical. In the present tense, the only difference is that the third person singular usually has an **s** on the end, whereas the plural and the first and second person singular do not: *I come, he comes, they come.* Exceptions to this are forms of the modal verbs, such as *can; may; will,* which do not have an **s** in the third person singular: *she can; he may*; and the verb *to be*, which has distinctive forms in the first and third person singular in both the present and the past tenses.

When two subject pronouns are joined by *or*, the verb should agree with the second. To find out more about this, see ◊compound subject.

-person In recent years this has been used as a suffix to avoid *-man* or *-woman*. It is useful for employers, who should not appear to be advertising specifically for a male or female employee, and also when the gender of the person is not known. For example, a pub owner may advertise for a *barperson*, but once the vacancy is filled the employer will refer to *the new barman* or *barmaid*.

Advertisers use similar words for jobs traditionally done by men, for which they expect only male applicants: *dustperson; milkperson; handyperson*. Such terms are seldom used otherwise, except in fun. When the gender of the person is known, -*person* nearly always refers to a woman; a man will be called a *chairman* or a *spokesman*, a woman is more likely to be referred to as a *chairperson* or *spokesperson*.

personnel Spelling: note the double **n**.

perspicacious See ◊perceptive.

perspicuous See ◊perceptive.

persuade See ◊convince.

pessimist Spelling: note the double **s** and single **m**.

pettiness Spelling: the **y** of *petty* changes to an **i**.

pharaoh Spelling: note the ending **-aoh**.

Philippines Spelling: remember the single **l** and double **p**.

phlegm Spelling: remember the silent **g**.

phoenix The pronunciation is [**fee**-niks].

pianissimo Spelling: note the double **s** and single **m**.

picaresque See ◊picturesque.

piccolo Spelling: remember the double **c** and single **l**.

picturesque *or* **picaresque** Picturesque relates to something pretty or attractive, especially in a quaint or charming way: *The filmmakers chose the village because of its picturesque setting*. **Picaresque** relates to a story that deals with the adventures of a likable rogue: *The novels* Kim *and* Huckleberry Finn *are not only similar in plan but are both picaresque, with a likable rogue of a boy as a traveller*.

pitiful, pitiable, *or* **piteous** Pitiful relates to someone or something that excites pity or is contemptible: *The aftermath of the fire was a pitiful sight, with many houses completely destroyed; Jessica's knowledge of geography is pitiful: she thought Athens was in Egypt*. **Pitiable** relates to a person or thing that is lamentable or wretched: *The* *old woman was in a pitiable plight, with no one to care for her*. **Piteous** is used for evidence of suffering and misery, evoking pity: *The crowds of undernourished and starving children were a piteous sight*.

placid Spelling: note there is only one **c**.

plague Spelling: remember the ending **-gue**.

plain See ◊plane.

plain English This is the kind of English to use in business: in letters, memos, reports to your colleagues, documents giving information to the public, promotional material, coursework and examination essays, or in any situation in which you are giving information, or want to persuade or interest.

Plain English is clear, concise, effective, interesting English. It saves time, paper, and misunderstanding, and so it saves money.

To make your English clear, you need to put yourself in the position of your reader, and decide what they need to know. In addition to the main facts, is there any background information you need to provide so that the reader can understand them? What is the most helpful way to order the information?

Show how your ideas are related. It may be obvious to you, but your readers will be happier if you give them signposts. Connect sentences with words and phrases such as *for example*; *however*; *on the other hand*; *but*; *besides*; *so*; *at first*; *secondly*; *in other words*; *in the first place*; *as a result*; *eventually*; *otherwise*.

If you need to deal with several questions, provide a clear heading for each.

Some information is very simple, and can be given in a straightforward way, but some is complicated. Would examples help? If the information is rather general, can you say what its practical implications are?

Write in everyday English. This will often save thinking time, for you can use the words that you first thought of when you got your aims straight for yourself. Don't waste time and lose clarity by wrapping up the plain facts in flowery language, long words, unnecessary technical terms, legalese, officialese, bureaucratic language, jargon, clichés, unnecessary words, or any other form of gobbledegook. Research shows that simple language sells products and services better than any other kind.

Don't waffle or pad. Be direct. Use *we* for your organization, rather than talking about it in the third person, and use *you* for the readers. For example, don't say, *The Sheffield and Manchester Building Society is endeavouring to develop a wider client base, and to this end is offering an attractive package to first time mortgage applicants.* Say, *If you are a first-time borrower, you pay a lower rate of interest.* Don't be pompous. That is, don't use phrases such as *not unmindful.*

In objective scientific writing there is good reason to use the passive, and to use long nouns made from verbs: *The leaves were classified; the classification of the leaves.* Who did the classifying is irrelevant. But where people matter, or emotions are involved, use active verbs rather than passive ones, and prefer the concrete to the abstract.

Keep sentences reasonably short, but not too short. Fifteen to twenty words is a good average. Don't be afraid to add a comma if it will make something clearer, particularly before *and.* What do you understand by the following sentence: *The articles were sorted by size and price labels attached.*

Did you start by thinking that the articles had been sorted according to size AND price, and then have to go back and re-analyze the sentence to see that *and* here joins two clauses and not two nouns? A comma before *and* would have prevented the confusion.

If you produce documents of which large numbers of copies go to the public, other companies, or government departments, you may like to have the help of Plain English Campaign, 'an independent organization which fights for clear, effective business communication and wants to stamp out all forms of gobbledegook.' For a fee, they will edit, write, and design documents, and train staff. They are particularly concerned with official documents and consumer contracts. They publish an *A-Z of alternative words*, plain English alternatives for words that make writing dull, confusing, or long-winded.

Plain English Campaign is at PO Box 3, New Mills, Stockport, SK12 4QP. Their telephone number is 01663 744409.

plainness Spelling: note the double **n**.

plane *or* **plain** Both words can apply to a flat or level area. A **plane** is a more or less technical term for a flat surface: *The sides of a pyramid rise on an inclined plane to meet at its apex; Joe tried to raise the level of conversation to a more elevated plane.* A **plain** is a level tract of country: *'A gentle knight was pricking on the plain'* (Spenser).

plaque Spelling: note the ending **-que**.

platypus Spelling: note the single **t** and single **s**.

playwright Spelling: remember that the second part is not **-write**.

plethora A *plethora of* is sometimes used to mean 'plenty of', 'a large selection of'. It actually means 'an excessive number or amount of': *a plethora of petty rules*.

pleural (meaning 'to do with the lungs'). Do not confuse this word with *plural*.

plimsoll *or* **plimsole** This word can be spelled either way.

plough US spelling: *plow*.

plumbing Spelling: remember the silent **b**.

Plurals

1. Most English plurals are formed by adding **s**.

2. Words that end in **-s**, **-sh**, **-ss**, **-tch**, or **-x**, add **es**:

gas → gases
dish → dishes
boss → bosses
watch → watches
box → boxes

3. For most words ending in **o**, add **es**:

hero → heroes
potato → potatoes
tomato → tomatoes

But many words just add **s**:

kilo → kilos
photo → photos
piano → pianos

In some cases either of these spellings is acceptable.

4. Most words ending in **-f** or **-fe** change the **f** to **v** and add **es**:

thief → thieves
half → halves
shelf → shelves
knife → knives
yourself → yourselves

There are some exceptions:

chief → chiefs
roof → roofs

With some words either form is acceptable:

handkerchief → handkerchiefs or handkerchieves
hoof → hoofs or hooves

5. Words ending in **y**, preceded by a consonant, change **y** to **i** and add **es**:

spy → spies
lady → ladies
ferry → ferries
opportunity → opportunities
penny → pennies

But for words where a vowel precedes the final **y**, you just add **s**:

day → days
monkey → monkeys
holiday → holidays
chimney → chimneys

6. There are some irregular plurals that don't follow any rule. For example:

ox → oxen
child → children
louse → lice
goose → geese
tooth → teeth

Some words have the same form in the plural:

aircraft → aircraft
sheep → sheep
series → series
species → species

7. Some words of foreign origin (mainly from Latin or French) have their own special plural forms:

-um → -a
-a → -ae
-us → -i

-is → -es

-eau → -eaux

So:

medium → media

formula → formulae

radius → radii

axis → axes

gateau → gateaux

pneumatic Spelling: remember the **p**.

pneumonia Spelling: remember the **p**.

poignant Spelling: remember the **gn**.

poltergeist Spelling: note the **ei**.

pomegranate Spelling: note the single **m**, and the ending **-ate**.

pore See ◊pour.

Portuguese Spelling: note the ending **-uese**.

possess Spelling: note the two double ss.

possessive pronoun a pronoun that indicates ownership of something. The possessive pronouns are: *mine; yours; his; hers; its; ours; their*.

potato Spelling: note there is no **e** at the end.

pour *or* **pore** To **pour** is to fall as liquid: *The rain poured down*. To **pore** is to study something intently: *We pored over the map, looking for the best route*. Despite the apparent common concept of downward direction, the two words are not related.

practical *or* **practicable** If something is **practical** it is useful and likely to be successful; if it is **practicable** it can be carried out, or put into practice: *You have made a practical suggestion, but I wonder if in this case it will be practicable?*

practice *or* **practise** Practice is the noun, and **practise** the verb (though not in the USA, when it is *practice*): *I'm afraid I'm rather out of practice; Why don't you practise what you preach?* See also ◊practical. To spell the two words correctly, remember *advice* (noun) and *advise* (verb).

practitioner Spelling: remember the two **ti**s.

pray *or* **prey** To **pray** is to 'talk' to your god; to **prey** on someone or something is to hunt, catch or exploit them: *I pray that it won't rain today*; *It's been preying on my mind for some time now*; *The praying mantis is so called not because it preys on living insects for its food but because when at rest it folds its front legs as if praying.*

precede See ◊proceed.

predilection Spelling: remember **-ile-**, not **-eli-**.

predominantly Spelling: *predomin-***ant-**ly (not **-ate-**ly).

prefix a group of letters that can be added to the beginning of a word to make a new word. For example, the prefix *over-* can be added to the word *charge* to make the word *overcharge*; the prefix *co-* can be added to the word *pilot* to make the word *co-pilot*.

prejudice Spelling: note that there is no **d** before the **j**.

premise *or* **premiss** **Premises** is the standard spelling for the words relating to buildings and to a reasoned idea: *The office premises are vacant*; *I am basing my premise on what you told me.* However, **premiss** is an alternative spelling for the second sense, especially in its use as a term in logic: *The two first parts of an argument in logic are known as the major premiss and the minor premiss.*

preposition This is a part of speech coming before a noun or a pronoun. A preposition can show location: *in; on*; time: *during*, or some other relationship, for example, figurative relationships in phrases like *by heart* or *in truthfulness*.

In the sentence *'Put the book on the table'*, *on* is a preposition governing the noun *table* and relates the verb *put* to the phrase *the table*, indicating where the book should go.

Many people know the 'rule' that says that a sentence should never end with a preposition. Traditional English grammar rules such as this were based on Latin grammar and as it is not possible to end a Latin sentence with a preposition, it was considered incorrect in English too. There is no other justification for the rule and it may safely be disregarded. Put the preposition where it sounds natural: *These people have no idea what they are talking about. Have you found those pages you were looking for?*

prerogative Spelling: note the first **r**.

prescribe *or* **proscribe** The two verbs are virtual opposites. To **prescribe** something is to recommend or authorize it: *The doctor* *prescribed a course of antibiotics*; *The laws prescribe a strict penalty for this offence*. To **proscribe** something is to ban it: *The import of pornographic material was proscribed by law*; *The new nationalist party was proscribed*.

presently In standard British English this means 'in a little while', 'before long'. In some dialects, in Scots, and in American English, it retains an older meaning 'now', 'at this time': *She's presently in Canada*. This can sometimes be confusing: an English person saying *she's visiting Canada presently* would mean that she is soon to visit Canada, an American would mean that she is there now. Use *soon* or *now* if there is a danger of being misunderstood.

pretence US spelling: *pretense*.

pretentious language See ◊clichés, pretentious language, and jargon and ◊plain English.

prettiness Spelling: the **y** of *pretty* changes to an **i**.

prevent *Prevent* is followed by *from* or by a possessive: *They prevented me from going* or *they prevented my going*. The former is more common, and is often preferable when the verb is followed by a noun: *We prevented the baby from falling* rather than *we prevented the baby's falling* (a listener could not tell whether there was one baby or more). Constructions such as *They prevented me going*; *we prevented the baby falling* are best avoided in formal writing, as some people consider them incorrect. They are very common in speech, and there is no reason not to say them.

preventive *or* **preventative** The words are often used interchangeably to denote whatever prevents something else happening or occurring, especially when it is undesirable. However, **preventative** is often applied to an actual object, especially in noun form, while **preventive** is mostly reserved for an abstract concept, and remains an adjective: *Preventive medicine regards vitamin C as an effective preventative against colds*.

prey See ◊pray.

primarily There are two common British pronunciations, [**prime**-ruhlee] and [prime-**mer**-rily]. Purists favour the first one. The second is also the US pronunciation.

principle *or* **principal** A **principle** is a firm belief or conviction that one has about something, or a rule or law about the way something

works: *It would be against my principles to do such a thing*;
*A thermometer works on the principle that mercury expands when warm
and contracts when cool*. A **principal** is the head of a college: *She became
Principal in 1991*. *Principle* is always a noun, but *principal* can also be an
adjective meaning 'main', or 'chief': *My principal objection is the cost.*

pristine This means 'in its original condition', 'unspoilt'. It has also
acquired the meaning 'clean', 'spotless', 'as if new': *a pristine white
handkerchief*. Some people still consider this to be incorrect, but it is
widely used and generally accepted.

privacy The preferred British pronunciation has a short **i** sound like
the **i** in *privet*, though some speakers say [**pry**-versee], which is also the
US pronunciation.

privilege Spelling: remember -**ile**-, not -**eli**- .

proceed *or* **precede** To **proceed** is to go forward, especially after
stopping or turning: *The parade then proceeded up the High Street*. To
precede is to go in front: *The parade was preceded by two majorettes,
tossing and twirling their batons.*

prodigy *or* **protégé** A **prodigy** is an unusually talented child:
*Mozart gained early fame as a prodigy, giving public performances of
his own compositions at the age of six*. A **protégé** is a (usually young)
person who is guided or helped by someone else, by implication usually
older or wiser (and wealthier): *He came to regard Justin as his protégé,
encouraging and advising him in his studies whenever he could.*

profession Spelling: note there is only one **f**.

professor Spelling: note the single **f** and double **s**.

program *or* **programme** Spell this word **program** when referring
to computers or computing, and also in American English. Use
programme for other senses such as 'television programme' or 'a
programme of events'.

prohibit See ◊forbid.

project The verb is stressed on the second syllable and has a weak first
syllable [pruh-**ject**]. The noun is stressed on the first syllable, [**prodge**-
ect] or sometimes [**proe**-ject].

prone See ◊prostrate ◊liable.

pronoun This is a part of speech that is used in place of a noun,
usually to save repetition of the noun. For example: *The people arrived*

around nine o'clock. They behaved as though we were expecting them.
Here, *they* and *them* are substitutes for repeating *the people*.

They, *them*, *he*, and *she* are **personal pronouns** (representing
people); *this/these*, and *that/those* are **demonstrative pronouns**
(demonstrating or pointing to something: *this book and not that book.*

Words like *that* and *who* can be **relative pronouns** in sentences like
She said that she was coming and *Tell me who did it* (relating one clause
to another). *Myself* and *himself* are **reflexive pronouns** (reflecting back
to a person, as in *He did it himself*).

pronunciation Note that the spelling has **-nun-** in the middle, and
that this is pronounced [nun] and not [noun].

prophecy *or* **prophesy** Remember that **prophecy** is a noun
(meaning 'a prediction') and **prophesy** is a verb (meaning 'to predict').

proportion This is often used to mean 'some': *A proportion of
travellers prefer to drive.* Constructions such as *large, small,* or *greater
proportion* would give a better idea of how many of the travellers are
involved. However, all these are longer, and no more informative, than
some; many; a few; most, and there is really no good reason to use them.

proscribe See ◊prescribe.

prostrate, prone, *or* **supine** Prostrate means lying face
downwards, often as the result of some accident or illness: *He was
knocked over and lay prostrate for some minutes before getting up.*
Prone means the same. It usually lacks the suggestion of being suddenly
struck down, however, although it can apply to patients in bed: *The
medical students were advised not to move patients from the prone
position unless it was absolutely necessary.* **Supine** is the opposite, and
means lying on one's back, face up: *The beach was full of sun
worshippers, supine on the sand.*

protagonist Some people still maintain that, as the Greek word from
which *protagonist* comes meant 'first actor', there may be only one
protagonist in any situation, and the word should not be used to mean
'supporter' or 'advocator': *a protagonist of gay rights.* However, this
use is widely accepted, and you need have no misgivings about it. Words
do change their meanings, especially as they move from one language to
another. If we allowed words only in their original senses, we would still
be using the word *treacle* for an antidote to a poisonous bite (this was the
earliest meaning in English, taken from French; *treacle* is ultimately
from a Greek word meaning 'wild animal').

protégé See ◊prodigy.

proved *or* **proven** Both are forms of the past participle of **to prove**. **Proved** is more common in British English: *She has proved her innocence*, but **proven** is often used as an adjective: *her proven innocence*.

The traditional English pronunciation of *proven* is [**proo**-v'n], and the Scottish pronunciation is [**proe**-v'n], but because English people have become familiar with the Scottish legal term 'not proven' they too sometimes pronounce the word [**proe**-v'n].

provided *and* **providing** These are used to refer to a condition that must be fulfilled before something else can take place: *Provided you've finished your work, you may go*; *Providing it doesn't rain, we'll have a picnic*. Either is correct, but some people feel that *provided* is more formal. Do not use either to mean simply 'if' in sentences like *We'd never have gone on the picnic if we'd known it was going to rain*.

psalm Spelling: remember the **p**.

pseudonym Spelling: remember the **p**.

pterodactyl Spelling: remember the **p**.

purposely *or* **purposefully** To do something **purposely** is to do it deliberately or on purpose: *Please don't move those books: I put them there purposely*. To do something **purposefully** is to do it with determination: *'Right, you naughty children, here I come!' he said, and strode purposefully into the garden*.

pyjamas US spelling: *pajamas*.

quantitative Spelling: remember the -ta-.

quantum leap In physics, *quantum* refers to a very small amount of energy, momentum, etc, but in general use **quantum leap** is often used for a sudden dramatic increase or advance, implying a very large movement. In physics, a *quantum jump* or *leap* means 'the abrupt transition of a particle or atom from one energy state to another', so *quantum leap* is perhaps best used for a sudden increase or advance which, although it may not be large, brings about a dramatic change: *The 'last straw' was a* quantum leap *as far as the camel's back was concerned*.

quasi The traditional pronunciation is [**kwayz**- eye] but some people say [**kwarz**-ee].

queasiness Spelling: the **y** of *queasy* changes to an **i**.

queer See ◊gay.

question See ◊beg the question.

question mark This is a punctuation mark (?) used to indicate an enquiry, placed at the end of a direct question: *Who is coming?* or an implied question: *This is my reward?*. A question mark is never needed at the end of an indirect question: *He asked us who was coming*, since this is a statement. To express doubt, a writer or editor may insert a question mark: *born in ? 1235*, often in brackets.

The question mark carries the force of a full stop (indeed it contains one) so it is incorrect to use them together.

questionnaire Spelling: remember the double **n**.

queue Spelling: remember the double **ue**.

quotation marks These are punctuation marks ('') which are also known as quotes, inverted commas, or speech marks. They are used in pairs to mark off dialogue or quoted matter in a text: *'Will you buy me a present, please?' asked Jane*; *Jane asked, 'Will you buy me a present, please?'*; *'Will you please,' Jane asked, 'buy me a present?'*

Whether the direct speech comes first, last, or is broken, the inverted commas must enclose only the words that the speaker actually utters. The punctuation marks are part of the speech; they must be inside the inverted commas: *'You said, "Go home!" Those were your very words. No wonder he's upset,' said Steven angrily. 'I said "Go home if you want." He didn't have to go,' replied John.* Here the reported speech within the dialogue and the dialogue itself can be distinguished by the use of single and double quotation marks.

Quotation marks are sometimes used to indicate the title of a play, a book, the name of a ship, and so on, but italics (or underlining) are normally used for these, and both may be omitted. Quotation marks may also be used to indicate that the writer is using the word in an unusual, often ironic, way: *He is one of these 'modern' young men – appalling manners and terrifying appearance.* In British English, single quotes are now more commonly used than double ones, and double quotes within single; in American English normal practice is the other way round.

rabid Two pronunciations are acceptable, [**rab**- id] and [**ray**-bid].

raccoon *or* **racoon** This word can be spelled either way.

racialist *or* **racist** The words are often used interchangeably but a distinction can be made. A **racialist** is someone who believes in the superiority of one race (usually white) over another (usually black or coloured), and who voices their views when surrounded (and outnumbered) by representatives of the 'other' race: *Many white racialists in South Africa were bitterly opposed to the release of the ANC leader Nelson Mandela.*

A **racist** is more of a theorist, believing that race is what determines a person's characteristics, so that some races are superior to others: *Critics remain divided regarding the extent to which Rudyard Kipling was or was not a racist.* The accepted pronunciation of both noun and adjective is [**ray**-sist], as the word comes from *race.* The pronunciation [**ray**-shist], probably formed by analogy with *racialist* or *fascist,* is generally regarded as incorrect.

rack *or* **wrack** Rack is used of something painful or harmful: *She lay still, racked with pain*; *He racked his brains but could not think of an answer*; *This country is going to rack and ruin.* **Wrack** is simply an alternative form of rack, but in the three examples quoted is rare (some would say wrong) in the first two senses and only fairly common in the third – *wrack and ruin.*

racket *or* **racquet** This word (meaning a piece of sports equipment) can be spelled either way.

racoon See ▷raccoon.

racquet See ▷racket.

raise See ▷rase.

rancorous Spelling: there is no **u** after the first **o** as there is in *rancour.*

rarefied Spelling: note the **e** in the middle, not **i**.

rase *or* **raze** This word (meaning to demolish) can be spelled either way. Do not confuse it with *raise* meaning to lift.

raspberry Spelling: remember the **p**.

rateable *or* **ratable** This word can be spelled either way.

ravage *or* **ravish** To **ravage** is to destroy or lay waste: *The storms ravaged the wood, uprooting many trees*. To **ravish** is to seize and carry off by force, and hence to rape (which originally meant carrying off a woman with the aim of forcing her to have sex): *The dog was living wild and farmers feared it could ravage their flocks*. From this bad 'carrying off' sense came the good one of 'transporting' with delight: *The visitors were ravished by the beauty of the landscape before them*.

raze See ♭rase.

realm Spelling: remember the **a**.

reason **Reason** is usually followed by *that* or *why*: *The reason that* (or *why*) *we left was that no one spoke to us*. You can also omit both: *the reason we left*. If *reason* is followed by a phrase without a verb, use *for*: *the reason for our departure*.

Note that the verb *to be* which introduces the reason is not followed by *because*: *The reason was that* (not because) *no one spoke*.

rebuff, rebut, refute, repudiate These look quite similar, and all have the basic meaning 'oppose', 'reject', but they are used differently. To **rebuff** someone is to snub or reject them: *We offered to help, but she rebuffed us*. **Rebut** and **refute** both mean 'prove to be false': *rebut* is applied to evidence or an accusation; *refute* can also refer to a statement or to the person making it, if it is proved that what they say is not true.

Refute is sometimes used to mean 'deny or contradict without argument or proof' (although many people think this is wrong), and in this sense it can be confused with **repudiate**, which means to reject the authority or validity of something: *He repudiated the accusation* (because it was invalid, there was no evidence for it). *Repudiate* can also mean 'refuse to have anything to do with something': *She repudiated all our offers of help*. In this meaning it overlaps with *rebuff*, but usually refers to the offers rather than the person making them.

recede Spelling: note the ending **-ede**.

receipt Spelling: remember the **ei**, and the silent **p**.

receive Spelling: remember the **ei** after **c**.

recommend Spelling: remember the single **c** and double **m**.

reconnaissance The stress is on the second syllable, and the word is pronounced [rick-**con**-uh-suhns]. Spelling: note the double **n** and double **s**.

recourse *or* **resort** A **resort** is something one turns to for help, especially when all else has failed: *As a last resort, I contacted the police*. The word is also a verb: *Whenever she had a headache, she would resort to lying on the bed with her eyes closed*. **Recourse** is the act of *resorting* to someone or something: *When roused, he would frequently have recourse to bad language*.

recurrent Spelling: note the double **r**, unlike *recur*.

redoubtable Spelling: remember the **b**.

referred Spelling: note the double **r**, unlike *refer*.

reflexive pronoun an object pronoun that refers to the same person as the subject: *I cut myself*; *You see yourself as the leader*. The other reflexive pronouns are *Himself, herself, itself, ourselves, yourselves, themselves*, and *oneself*.

refrigerator Spelling: remember no **d** before the **g**.

refute See ▷rebuff.

regardless See ▷irrespective.

register office *or* **registry office** Both are widely used, and neither can be regarded as incorrect. However, **register office** is the official term, and should be used in formal speech and writing.

regretfully *or* **regrettably** **Regretfully** means 'feeling or showing regret', **regrettably** means 'undesirable', 'causing regret', 'open to criticism'. *Regrettably* is sometimes used in place of *regretfully*, but this should be avoided because of the difference in meaning: *Regretfully, he declined their invitation* means that he was, or appeared to be, full of sadness and regret at having to do so. *Regrettably, he declined their invitation* means that his refusal is something to regret; perhaps because he had no good reason for doing so or because things would have turned out better if he had accepted.

reign *or* **rein** To **reign** is to rule, while to **rein** is to check. Hence the expression *give free rein* (not *reign*), meaning to allow freedom to someone or something when it might otherwise have been held in check (like a horse by its reins): *She gave the gardener free rein to work as he thought best*; *Judy gave free rein to her imagination about what she would do if she won the pools.*

relative clause Relative clauses are clauses which modify what they are attached to – that is to say, they affect its meaning in some way. Most relative clauses modify a noun. In this way they act rather like adjectives – in fact *adjectival clause* is another name for them. There are two types of these: restrictive relative clauses (also called defining relative clauses) and non-restrictive relative clauses (also called non-defining relative clauses).

Restrictive relative clauses identify and particularize the noun they modify, and the sentence would be incomplete without them: *The zebra which the lion picked on was clearly sick.* They can be introduced by the relative pronouns *who, whom, whose* or *which,* or by *that*: *The zebra that the lion picked on was clearly sick.* They can also be used without a relative pronoun: *The zebra the lion picked on was clearly sick.* You do not put a comma before and after them.

Non-restrictive relative clauses merely give additional information about the noun, which is dispensable: *The zebra, which lives in southern Africa, is related to the horse.* They can only be introduced by *who, whom, whose* and *which*, never by *that.* You generally put a comma before a non-restrictive relative clause (and after it, if it does not end the sentence).

There is a third sort of relative clause, which modifies not a noun but a whole clause: *They can't come after all, which is a shame.* It can only be introduced by *which.*

renege The standard pronunciation is [ri-**neeg**], though some British speakers say [ri-**naig**].

repertoire *or* **repertory** A **repertoire** is properly the range of acts, songs, turns, and the like that a particular company or actor can perform, and hence anyone's 'stock' of similar things: *Uncle Geoff has a good repertoire of corny jokes.* A **repertory** can be the same, but the word usually refers more precisely to the plays that a company performs at one theatre over a period: *Many famous performers started their career in repertory companies.* Spelling: remember the second **r**.

replica A **replica** is a model of something, but it is a particular kind of model and the two words are not interchangeable. A *model* may represent a type of thing rather than a specific example: *a model railway,* and it may be quite crude and not very much like the original: *a pink plastic model of the Taj Mahal*. A model may be of something which does not yet exist: engineers sometimes make detailed scale models of things they are planning or constructing. A **replica** is an exact copy of a specific thing which exists or has existed in the past, and is usually made to scale.

repudiate See ▷rebuff.

rescind The **c** is not pronounced, and the stress is on the second syllable. The first syllable is the same as the beginning of *return*. Spelling: remember the **c**.

research The standard pronunciation of both verb and noun in Britain, especially among researchers, has the stress on the second syllable [ri-**search**], but a pronunciation with the stress on the first syllable [**ree**-search] is gaining ground among the general public. The situation is the same in the US, except that the **r** is pronounced.

resign Spelling: remember the **g**.

resort See ▷recourse.

restaurant Spelling: remember the **au**.

restaurateur Note that, unlike *restaurant*, this is spelt and pronounced without an **n**.

resurrection Spelling: note the single **s** and double **r**.

resuscitate Spelling: remember the **sc**.

retch See ▷wretch.

review *or* **revue** A **review** is a re-examination, survey, or report: *This schedule is subject to review*; *Most company reports include a financial review of the year*; *I quite agreed with the review of the TV programme*. A **revue** (the French equivalent) is a theatrical entertainment, either of song and dance, and purely for pleasure, or satirical in some way: *After the war many spectacular revues turned into night club or strip-tease shows*; *One of the first great TV satirical revues was 'That Was the Week that Was'*.

rhapsody Spelling: remember the **h**.

rheumatism Spelling: remember the **h**.

rhinoceros Spelling: remember the **h** and the ending **-os**.

rhombus Spelling: remember the **h**.

rhyme Spelling: remember the **hy**.

rhythm Spelling: remember the **hy**.

rigid Spelling: there is no **d** before the **g**.

rigorous Spelling: there is no **u** before the second **r**, unlike *rigour*.

risotto Spelling: note the single **s** and double **t**.

rogue Spelling: remember the ending **-gue**.

rural *or* **rustic** **Rural** is to do with the country or countryside, as opposed to the town: *Rural amenities are inevitably more basic than urban ones*; *Teresa loved the peaceful rural setting of the place*. **Rustic** is to do with the country as being characteristically simple, quaint, or attractive: *I sat for a while on the rustic seat under the oak*; *The couple lived in rustic simplicity in a little village*.

saccharin *or* **saccharine** Saccharin is an artificial sweetener whereas **saccharine** means something excessively sweet: *a saccharine smile*. Spelling: remember the double **c**.

sachet Spelling: remember the ending **-et**.

sacrament Spelling: remember **a** in the middle, not **e**.

sacrilegious Spelling: remember **-ile-**, not **-eli-**. The word is related to *sacrilege*, not *religious*.

Sagittarius Spelling: note the single **g** and double **t**.

sake, saké, *or* **saki** This word can be spelled in all three ways.

salmon Spelling: remember the **l**.

satellite Spelling: note the single **t** and double **l**.

sauciness Spelling: the **y** of *saucy* changes to an **i**.

Saudi The standard current pronunciation is [**sow**-dee]. A few people still use an older pronunciation [**sore**-dee], and people who have dealings with Saudi Arabia sometimes pronounce it more like Arabs do, and say [sar-**oo**-dee].

scallop The standard pronunciation in Britain is [**skol**-op], to rhyme with *trollop*. Some people pronounce it, as you might expect from the spelling, with a short **a** sound. This is the standard pronunciation in the USA, although [**skol**-op] is also heard there. Note that the word can also be spelt *scollop*. In this case it is pronounced as you would expect from the spelling.

scantiness Spelling: the **y** of *scanty* changes to an **i**.

scenario A scenario is a state of affairs that may come about, or a series of events that may happen. It is often used in the context of planning to deal with such an eventuality: *In this scenario, unemployment has reached five million. What action should be taken?* Avoid using it to mean 'plan' or 'scheme'. It has recently been somewhat overused: it may sometimes be better to use words such as *prediction; projection; development; outlook,* or *prospect.*

sceptic US spelling: *skeptic.*

sceptical See ◊cynical.

sceptre Spelling: remember the **c**.

schedule The usual British pronunciation is [**shed**-youl], but the US pronunciation [**sked**-youl] is increasingly heard in Britain.

scheme Spelling: remember the **sch**.

schism The standard current pronunciation is [**skizz**-um], though traditionalists and clergymen still frequently use [**sizz**-um].

schizophrenic Spelling: remember the **sch**.

scholar Spelling: remember the **sch**.

science Spelling: remember the **sc**.

scissors Spelling: remember the **sc**.

scone Both [skon] and [skone] are heard in Britain, with [skon] probably more common. The standard US pronunciation is [skone], though [skahn] is also heard.

scorch Spelling: there is no **t** before the **ch**.

Scottish, Scots, *or* **Scotch** Scottish is generally applied to things: *Scottish scenery; Scottish education; the Scottish Office.* **Scots** is generally applied to people: *a Scots girl.* This is not a rigid distinction; many Scots would not object to being called Scottish, and some things felt to be closely associated with people may have either form: *Scots* (or Scottish) *law.*

Scots, as a noun, is the name of the form of English spoken in Scotland, particularly in the Lowlands. **Scotch** was once widely used of Scottish things or people; it is now very limited, applied to things which got their names before it fell out of general use: *Scotch broth; Scotch egg; Scotch* (now sometimes called Scottish) *terrier.* As a noun, it refers only to whisky.

scourge Spelling: remember the **ou**.

scrimmage, scrummage, *or* **scrum** A scrimmage is any general confused tussle or struggle, as also is a **scrum** (though perhaps a more local one): *There was a real scrimmage outside the store before the* *sales, and a scrum round the bargain counter as soon as the doors opened.* A **scrummage** (or *scrum*) is a set formation in Rugby football.

scruffiness Spelling: the **y** of *scruffy* changes to an **i**.

scrum See ◊scrimmage.

scrummage See ◊scrimmage.

scythe Spelling: remember the **c**.

seasonal *or* **seasonable** If something is **seasonal**, it relates to a particular season (often summer): *He got seasonal work hiring out deck chairs on the beach.* If a thing is **seasonable** it is appropriate for the season or occasion: *The snow was unexpected but seasonable for the time of year.*

secede The stress is on the second syllable [sis- **seed**]. Spelling: remember the ending **-ede**.

secretary The standard British pronunciation has only three syllables [**seck**-ruh-tree]. The US pronunciation has four [**seck**-ruh-ter-ry]. Note that the pronunciation [**seck**-ertree] is considered wrong.

seize Spelling: note the **ei**.

self-deprecating See ◊deprecate.

selvage *or* **selvedge** This word can be spelled either way.

semicolon This is a punctuation mark (;) with a function halfway between the separation of sentence from sentence by means of a full stop, and the weaker separation provided by a comma. It also helps separate items in a complex list: *pens, pencils, and paper; staples, such as rice and beans; tools, various; and rope.*

    Rather than the abrupt *We saw Mark last night. It was good to see him again*, and the grammatically inaccurate *We saw Mark last night, it was good to see him again*, the semicolon reflects a link in a two-part statement and is considered good style: *We saw Mark last night; it was good to see him again.* An alternative in such cases is to use a comma followed by *and* or *but*.

sensual *or* **sensuous** Sensual usually relates to physical and specifically sexual pleasures: *She delighted in the sensual warmth of the sun; He observed the sensual sway of her hips.* **Sensuous** relates to something that appeals to the senses (sight, smell, hearing, touch, taste), especially when it is luxurious: *There was a scent of new-mown hay, warm and sensuous; She ran her sensuous fingers down his arm.*

separate Spelling: remember **-par-** not **-per-** in the middle.

sergeant Spelling: remember **ser,** not **sar.**

sexism in language

In recent decades feminists have become concerned that certain usages in English suggest outdated or unfair beliefs about the roles that men and women have or could have in society. More and more people have come to sympathize. They want to avoid language which is thought to discriminate against women, and expressions which encourage stereotypical images of men and women. Many writers who do not feel strongly about such issues nonetheless wish to avoid offending those who do. Some employers have a code of practice that requires that such language should be avoided, and equal opportunities legislation requires employers to offer a job without requiring that applicants for it should be of a particular sex.

1. Man/humanity

A practice that especially offends is the use of **man** to mean 'people in general'. Studies have shown that when people meet sentences such as *It was at this period that man began to keep domestic animals*, many have mental images of men only, and not of women. Another problem is that a writer may start out using *man* to mean 'people in general, both men and women', but then drift into its other sense of 'males', with a sentence such as *Among man's most basic needs are food, shelter, and a woman to be the mother of his children.* You have only to look at a sentence such as *Like all mammals, man breastfeeds his young*, to see that *man* is not really an all-purpose neutral term for humankind. There are various ways of avoiding this problem. For example, instead of saying *God and Man*, you could say *God and Humans*. Here are some suggestions for alternatives.

Instead of	Use
mankind, man	people, humans, human beings, humanity, humankind, the human race, the human species, society, men and women
man	human being, human, person, individual
man's nature	human nature
the man in the street	the average person, ordinary people
man hours	work hours
manpower	workforce, staff, workers
man-made	artificial, synthetic, manufactured
man-to-man	personally, person-to-person
manned by	staffed by

2. Man/person

The use of *man/men* to mean 'individual humans' is another to avoid. *Person/people* is the most frequently used substitute, and often works well.

Many job titles have the ending *-man*. Some people favour simply substituting the ending *-person* in all such cases. Some of these words, *barperson* for example, have become established in job advertisements. Others, such as *postperson*, still sound strange to most people, and are the subject of jokes. Sometimes perfectly acceptable alternatives that are neither sexist nor odd already exist. Here are some examples.

Instead of	Use
businessman	executive
cameraman	camera operator
charlady	cleaner
fireman	firefighter
foreman	supervisor
headmaster	head, head teacher
headmistress	head, head teacher
policeman	police officer
statesman	leader, politician

Chairman is a notorious case of the *-man* ending. In the past it was used for women as well as for men. *Chairwoman* was also used for a woman. But the need is for a neutral term in which sex is not shown. And there are, of course, many occasions when you do not know the sex of the person, for example, *Who's going to be the next – ?* Feminists have proposed *chairperson* and *chair*, and these are becoming increasingly common, although they annoy many people who dislike political correctness. You can sometimes avoid offending anyone by rephrasing. Instead of saying, *The chair will be Elizabeth Williams*, you can simply say, *The chair will be taken by Elizabeth Williams*, or *Elizabeth Williams will be in the chair*.

3. He

One of the most difficult problems is the lack of a singular personal pronoun with which to refer to one person whose sex is unknown or irrelevant. Traditionally *he* has been used, with *his* as the possessive, but the use of these is open to the same objection as the use of *man*. Solutions are:

Change to a plural, so that: *A customer who fails to pay will find his wheels clamped when he tries to leave* becomes: *Customers who fail to pay will find their wheels clamped when they try to leave.*

Use *they* and *their* for the singular, so that: *If a student can't be in class, he'll have to do the work in his own time* becomes: *If a student can't be in class, they'll have to do the work in their own time.* This is a usage that is well established in informal spoken English. For more on this use, see ◊they.

Use a relative, so that: *If someone parks in the wrong bay, he will be banned from the car park* becomes: *Anyone who parks in the wrong bay will be banned from the car park.*

Use the imperative, so that: *Each driver must carry his licence on him* becomes: *Carry your licence on you.*

Use an article instead of a possessive, so that: *a person who takes his car into central London* becomes: *a person who takes a car into central London.*

Avoid the need for the pronoun by rephrasing what you have to say, so that: *Ask the nurse to help you, but if she can't...* becomes: *Ask the nurse to help you, but if this isn't possible...*

Use *he or she*, *his or her*, and *his or hers*, though you should avoid using these structures repeatedly because they can become rather cumbersome.

Use *s/he*. This is effective in written rules, etc, but cannot be used in speech.

4. Feminine forms
Many people object to feminine forms of job titles, and they are used less and less.

Instead of	Use
authoress	author
comedienne	comedian
conductress	conductor
manageress	manager
poetess	poet
sculptress	sculptor
steward	flight attendant
stewardess	flight attendant

Make an effort to avoid assuming that people who do a particular job are necessarily male or necessarily female. Do not call doctors who are women *lady doctors*. You would not call doctors who are men *men doctors*.

Do not use *girl* for older women. Use it only where the masculine equivalent is *boy*. Otherwise, it can sound patronising. Similarly, only use *lady* when you would use *gentleman* if talking about a man.

5. Mrs/Miss/Ms

Many women object to having to be labelled as married or unmarried when they give their title as *Mrs* or *Miss*. Men are all *Mr* and do not have to reveal their marital status. Feminists proposed *Ms* as a female equivalent of *Mr*, and it is now well established as an option.

There is an increasing tendency towards dropping all titles and using a person's first name and surname in letters, public notices, and so on. If you are writing to someone such as a company's customer care officer, and you do not know the name or sex of that person, start the letter *Dear Sir or Madam*. See also ◊chair, ◊girl, ◊he, ◊lady, ◊man, ◊Ms, ◊- person, ◊they, ◊woman.

shabbiness Spelling: the **y** of *shabby* changes to an **i**.

shall *or* will *Shall* and *will* are both used as auxiliary verbs to form the future tense. In standard British English, the traditional difference between the two is that **shall** is used with *I* and *we*: *I shall leave* and **will** is used with nouns and *you, he, she, it* and *they*: *You will stay*. In practice, though, *shall* is going out of use in this role, and *will* is widely used for the first person: *I will leave*. This is now widely accepted as part of standard English. In American English, *will* is the norm in all persons for the future tense.

A parallel development has been the gradual decline of *will* in the first person and *shall* in the second and third persons to express determination, promises or commands. *I will leave* now indicates merely intention, not, as in the past, determination; and usages like *Cinderella, you shall go to the ball* now sound rather old-fashioned.

The first person *shall* does survive as a way of making a suggestion or asking a question: *Shall I put the light on?* means 'Would you like me to put the light on?', not 'Am I going to put the light on?'

shapeliness Spelling: the **y** of *shapely* changes to an **i**.

sheik *or* sheikh This word can be spelled either way. The current standard pronunciation is [shake], but older people sometimes still use [sheek].

shepherd Spelling: remember the **h**.

sheriff Spelling: remember the single **r** and double **f**.

shiftiness Spelling: the **y** of *shifty* changes to an **i**.

shininess Spelling: the **y** of *shiny* changes to an **i**.

shoddiness Spelling: the **y** of *shoddy* changes to an **i**.

should *or* **would** The main use of **should** is to mean 'ought to': *You shouldn't speak like that to your mother*. It is also used after *if* to express hypothetical situations: *If it should rain, the performance will be indoors* and after *that* in expressing suggestions, arrangements and necessities: *I suggested that he should leave*. See ◊subjunctive.

Would is used in conditional sentences: *If it weren't so expensive, I would buy it*; in reporting the words of someone who has said *will*: *She said she would let me know tomorrow*; and to say what used to happen: *Every evening he would go along to the pub*.

Formerly, *should* replaced *would* after *I* and *we* in the first two of these three uses: *If it weren't so expensive, I should buy it*. In present-day English, however, this sounds rather old-fashioned, and it is preferable to use *would*. There are, though, certain expressions, such as *I should think* and *I shouldn't wonder*, in which it is still the norm to use *should*.

sieve Both the noun and the verb are pronounced [siv]. [Seev] is not standard.

silhouette Spelling: remember the **h**.

silicon *or* **silicone** **Silicon** is the non-metallic chemical element used for making microchips: *The Santa Clara valley, in California, is known as Silicon Valley because many of the country's leading computer firms are located there*. **Silicone** is a compound made from *silicon* that has various domestic and surgical applications: *Silicone has been widely used as a plastic in breast implants*.

silliness Spelling: the **y** of *silly* changes to an **i**.

sincerely Spelling: remember the second **e**.

singular or plural verb? As a rule, singular nouns and pronouns go with a singular verb and plural nouns and pronouns go with a plural verb. However, there are some exceptions to this rule in English. To find out more about them, look at the entries for ◊collective noun, ◊compound subject, ◊number and ◊they/their/theirs.

situation *Situation*, in the sense 'state of affairs' is often used in unnecessarily long-winded phrases: *This is a crisis situation*; *We are in a no-win situation*. *This is a crisis* and *we cannot win* are simpler and more elegant. Avoid using *situation* to mean 'problem': *the problem of homelessness* rather than: *the homelessness situation.*

skein This is pronounced [skane] to rhyme with *pain*. Spelling: note the **ei**.

skilful Spelling: note the single **ls**.

slander See ◊libel.

sleigh Spelling: note the **ei**.

sleight This is pronounced to rhyme with *height*. Spelling: remember **ei** not **ie**.

smoulder US spelling: *smolder*.

sobriquet This is a sophisticated word for nickname or unofficial name. The pronunciation reflects its French origin and is [so-**brick**-kay]. The US pronunciation of the first syllable is [soo]. Spelling: note the ending **-quet**.

social *or* **sociable** **Social** relates to society in some way: *I'm not doing this out of a sense of social duty*; *The two children were friends although each came from quite a different social background.* **Sociable** relates to the enjoyment of company: *She was a sociable old lady, and always liked a good chat*; *'Society is no comfort/To one not sociable'* (Shakespeare).

soldier Spelling: note there is no **j** in it.

solecism *or* **solipsism** A **solecism** is a mistake in the use of language, or more generally an offence against good manners or etiquette: *To say 'seasonal' when you mean 'seasonable' is a solecism. Pouring tea from your cup into the saucer to cool it is a solecism.* **Solipsism** is the theory that there can be no existence apart from one's own: *Solipsism is an extreme form of subjective idealism.*

solemn Spelling: remember the **n**.

solipsism See ◊solecism.

somersault Spelling: note the **o** and the single **m**.

sort See ◊kind.

soulless Spelling: note the double **l**.

sovereign Spelling: note the **ei** and the **g**.

spaghetti Spelling: remember the **h**.

speciality US spelling: *specialty*.

spectre
Spelling: note the ending **-re**, although the US spelling is **-er**.

spelling rules

1. Doubling letters
Some people are unsure whether to double the last letter of a word when adding suffixes like **-ed**, **-ing**, or **-er** to the word. Below are a number of simple rules.

• Most short words of one syllable ending with a single consonant double the last letter:

tap → tapped
hit → hitting
shop → shopper

Words ending with more than one consonant don't double the last letter:

thump → thumped
halt → halting

• Words of more than one syllable ending with a single consonant double the last letter if the word is stressed on the last syllable:

begin → beginner
commit → committed
occur → occurring
prefer → preferring

If the stress is not on the last syllable, but an earlier one, the last letter is not doubled:

benefit → benefited
gallop → galloping
pardon → pardoned
offer → offering

Exceptions:
handicap → handicapped
kidnap → kidnapper
worship → worshipping

• Words of more than one syllable ending in l double the l even if the stress does not fall on the last syllable:

cancel → cancelled
travel → travelling
jewel → jeweller

(These words take a single l in US spelling)

Exceptions:
appealing, paralleled.

• Final consonants are not doubled before suffixes beginning with a consonant:

enrol → enrolment
commit → commitment
fulfil → fulfilment
prefer → preferment
quarrel → quarrelsome
rival → rivalry

2. Keep *e*?
Some people are unsure whether to keep the final silent **e** of words when adding suffixes like **-ed**, **-ing**, **-er**, or **-ly**.

• If the suffix begins with a vowel, the **e** is dropped:

hope → hoping
dive → diver
pursue → pursuing
celebrate → celebrated

Exception:
age → ageing

• If the suffix begins with a consonant, the **e** is kept:

bare → barely
fine → finely
woe → woeful
refine → refinement
care → careless

Exceptions:
argue → argument
awe → awful

due → duly
true → truly
whole → wholly

3. *y* or *i*?

Some people are unsure whether to change **y** at the end of a word to **i**, when adding **-ed**, **-ing**, or **-er**.

• Words ending in **y** and preceded by a vowel, keep the **y**:

key → keying
play → playing
annoy → annoying

• Words ending in **y** and preceded by a consonant, change the **y** to **i** when adding **-ed** or **-er**:

cry → cried
fly → flier
carry → carried
dusty → dustier

But keep the **y** when adding **-ing**:

cry → crying
fly → flying
carry → carrying

4. *-ful* or *-full*?

Full becomes **-ful** when added to the end of a word:

beautiful
joyful
useful
mouthful
spoonful

Note also:
fulfil
fulfilment

But:
fullness

5. Adding *mis-* and *dis-*

When adding **mis-** or **dis-** to the beginning of a word, there is only one s unless the word itself begins with s:

misheard
disagree
disappear
misspelt
disservice
dissimilar

6. Adding *in-* and *un-*

When adding **in-** or **un-** to the beginning of a word, there is only one **n** unless the word itself begins with **n**:

inseparable
unending
innumerable
unnecessary

7. *i* before *e* except after *c*

• Most people know the rule *i before e except after c*. This rule works with many words, especially if the sound is **ee**:

ceiling
believe
deceive
niece
receive
shield
siege

Exceptions (examples):
seize
protein
weird
species
Keith
Neil
Sheila

• If the sound is **ay** the spelling is always **ei**:

freight
neighbour
weigh

8. Adding -*ly*

When -**ly** is added to a word ending in **y**, the **y** changes to an **i**:

happy → happily
necessary → necessarily

9. -*ize* or -*ise*?

In British English, many verbs can be spelt either -**ize** or -**ise**. -**ize** is the usual US spelling. Note capsize, prize (to value) which must be spelt -**ize**.

• Words spelt -**ise**: Note that these words can only be spelt -**ise**; there is no choice in the matter:

Nouns

compromise	franchise
demise	merchandise
disguise	revise
enterprise	surmise
exercise	surprise

Verbs

advertise	enterprise
advise	excise
apprise	exercise
arise	improvise
chastise	incise
circumcise	merchandise
comprise	premise
compromise	prise (open)
demise	revise
despise	supervise
devise	surmise
disguise	surprise
enfranchise	televise

10. -*able* or -*ible*?

It is not always easy to remember whether a word ends with -**able** or -**ible**. Most words end -**able**, and whenever new words are coined, they are usually spelt -**able**. There is no simple rule (it depends on the Greek or Latin word from which the word comes), but the set of commonly used words that end -**ible** is a fairly small one:

accessible
audible
collapsible
combustible
compatible
comprehensible
contemptible
convertible
credible
crucible
defensible
digestible
discernible
edible
eligible
fallible
feasible
flexible
forcible
gullible
horrible
inadmissible
incorrigible
incorruptible
indelible

indestructible
indivisible
inexhaustible
inexpressible
intelligible
invincible
irascible
irrepressible
irresistible
legible
negligible
ostensible
perceptible
permissible
plausible
possible
reducible
reprehensible
responsible
reversible
sensible
susceptible
tangible
terrible
visible

Most other adjectives end in **-able**.

spiciness Spelling: the **y** of *spicy* changes to an **i**.

spinach Spelling: there is no **t** before the **ch**.

split infinitive The infinitive is the basic form of a verb, with no added endings in English. For example, *come* in *Can you come?* is an infinitive. English often uses *to* with an infinitive, as in *I'd like to come*, and *to* has come to be regarded as part of the infinitive.

Grammarians in the 17th and 18th centuries, formulating the 'rules' of English grammar, based their views on the structure of Latin, which was considered to represent the high point of linguistic development. In Latin, the infinitive consists of a single word ('to come', for instance, is *venire*), which self-evidently cannot be interrupted by another word. These English grammarians therefore decided that the English two-

word infinitive should not be interrupted by another word either, and
their injunction against the *split infinitive* survives to the present time:
'Do not insert an adverb or adverbial phrase between to and the
following verb'.

The tenuous basis of the ban has been pointed out often enough for
most people to be aware of it, but the prejudice against the *split infinitive*
seems to be firmly embedded in English speakers' psyche. So, should
one split or not split?

Perhaps the most important point to make is that there are some
contexts in which it is virtually impossible not to split the infinitive, and
that in those cases you should go ahead and do so rather than produce a
nonsensical sentence. For example, *We've been asked to more than
triple our contribution*, although it contains a split infinitive, is at least a
well-formed English sentence; *We've been asked more than to triple our
contribution* is ungrammatical.

A particular danger of forcibly unsplitting an infinitive is that it can
change the meaning of the sentence. For instance, *She asked me to
kindly close the door* clearly indicates that she said, 'Kindly close the
door'. If you eliminate the split infinitive you get either: *She asked me
kindly to close the door*, which could mean something entirely different,
or: *She kindly asked me to close the door*, which certainly does.

Apart from cases like this, where comprehensibility and clarity call
for a split infinitive, splitting is a matter of personal preference. Do it if
you want to, but be aware that it annoys some people. Try to avoid a very
long adverbial phrase or string of adverbs between *to* and the verb,
which generally produces an inelegant effect: *It has been decided to
finally and with immediate effect close the swimming pool.*

Remember that in formal writing, where grammatical
conservativeness is the norm, there is more of a case for not splitting
infinitives than in everyday writing and speech. But even there, try to
avoid the thumping unsplit infinitive with the adverb in front of the *to*,
the sort which says 'Look at me, I'm not splitting the infinitive!': *The
government has promised seriously to consider the proposals* draws
attention to its own structure; *The government has promised to consider
the proposals seriously* is structurally unobtrusive, and allows us to
concentrate on its meaning. Take account of the rhythm and balance of
the sentence when deciding whether to split the infinitive; don't just do
it, or not do it, dogmatically.

Linguistic insecurity can lead people to avoid structures which they
mistakenly think are split infinitives. There is no need, for instance, to

contort *The talks are said to have completely collapsed* into *The talks are said completely to have collapsed*, because *completely* does not come between *to* and *have*, and this is therefore not an example of a split infinitive.

spokesperson See ◊-person.

sponsor Spelling: note the ending **-or**.

spoonful Spelling: note the single **l**.

sprightliness Spelling: the **y** of *sprightly* changes to an **i**.

squalid Spelling: note the single **l**.

squalor Spelling: note the ending **-or**.

staccato Spelling: note the double **c**.

stalactite *or* **stalagmite** A **stalactite** is an icicle-shaped formation of lime that hangs down from a cave roof. A **stalagmite** is the opposite, and extends upwards like a pillar from a cave floor: *A stalagmite grows higher as the water from a stalactite drips onto it*. One way of remembering which is which is to remember **t** for top and **t** in *stalactite*.

stammer *or* **stutter** To **stammer** is to speak with difficulty, hesitating, and repeating words: *'I can't – can't – don't know how to thank you,' he stammered*. To **stutter** is also to speak with difficulty, but typically involves repeating a single letter rather than a whole word: *'B-b-but you s-s-said you'd t- t-tell me,' she stuttered*.

stanch *or* **staunch** As a verb, this word can be spelled either way: *She managed to stanch* (or staunch) *the flow of blood*. As an adjective, however, only **staunch** is used: *He was a staunch supporter of the party*.

Standard English The form of English that in its grammar, syntax, vocabulary, and spelling system does not identify the speaker or the writer with a particular geographical area or social grouping. The accent associated with Standard English is known as 'received pronunciation' or RP.

stationary *or* **stationery** Stationary is used for a person or thing that is not moving: *The train was stationary in the station*. **Stationery** is writing materials, as supplied by a stationer: *There was plenty of paper in the office stationery store*. (Stationers are so called as at one time they had a regular stall, so were stationary, unlike other tradesmen, who travelled with their goods.) To remember how to spell these words, think of **e** for 'letter' (stationery) and **a** for 'car' (stationary).

status The standard pronunciation, both in Britain and the USA, is [**stay**-tus], though [**statt**-us] is also used.

staunch See ◊stanch.

steadiness Spelling: the **y** of *steady* changes to an **i**.

stealth Spelling: remember the **a**.

sternness Spelling: note the double **n**.

stickiness Spelling: the **y** of *sticky* changes to an **i**.

stiletto Spelling: note the single **l** and double **t**.

stinginess Spelling: the **y** of *stingy* changes to an **i**.

storey Note that this word (a floor of a building) is spelled *story* in American English.

straight *or* **strait** **Straight** is used of something direct, or continuing on an undeviating course: *The road ran straight for three miles*. **Strait**, a much rarer word, is used of something tight or confining, usually in set phrases or word combinations: *He said he'd try to keep on the strait and narrow*; *The mental patient had to be confined in a strait jacket*; *Aunt Dora was not at all strait-laced*.

stress The main emphasis, placed on any syllable of a spoken word. Stress patterns vary from word to word but follow certain rules.

stupefy Spelling: note the **e**, not **i** as in *stupid*.

stupor Spelling: note the ending **-or**.

sturdiness Spelling: the **y** of *sturdy* changes to an **i**.

stutter See ◊stammer.

stye *or* **sty** This word (meaning a swelling on the eyelid) can be spelled either way.

subject The noun, noun phrase, or pronoun that the sentence is about. For example: *The black dog* in *The black dog chased the brown dog*, and *The man* in *The man was injured by stampeding horses*.

subjunctive The subjunctive is a set of forms of a verb which express states that do not exist. There are two sorts of subjunctive in English: the present subjunctive and the past subjunctive. In form, the present subjunctive is the same as the infinitive, so the present subjunctive of *to be* is: *I be, you be, he/she/it be, we be, they be*. There is no *s* on the end of the third person singular: *he go; she leave; it have*.

The **present subjunctive** has three uses in modern English. First, it follows verbs, nouns or adjectives that express the idea of command, suggestion or possibility: *I suggested that he leave*; *It is my recommendation that she not be appointed*; *It is fitting that she resign*.

This use of the present subjunctive is common in American English. In British English it is more usual to use *should*: *I suggested that he should leave*, but it seems that the present subjunctive may be on the increase.

Second, it is used in formal English in clauses beginning with words such as *if; although; whether* and *lest*: *If that be the case, there is little more we can do*; *Tie her up securely, lest she escape*.

This use of the present subjunctive tends to sound stilted and old-fashioned, and in everyday speech and writing the indicative is usually used instead: *If that is the case...*, but again American English uses it more readily than British English.

Third, it is used in certain fixed phrases, such as *far be it from me; be that as it may; God save the Queen; come what may; suffice it to say; heaven forbid; perish the thought*.

The **past subjunctive** effectively relates only to the verb *to be*, where it takes the form *were*. It is used to express hypothetical states, and comes after the verbs *wish* and *suppose*, conjunctions such as *if; if only; as; though; whether*, and the phrases *would rather* and *would that*: *I wish she were here*; *If I were you, I'd resign*; *Would that he were still alive.*

It is widely used in everyday English, but in non-formal contexts it is often replaced by *was* in the first and third person singular: *I wish she was here.* In formal or literary English, the order of *if*-clauses can be reversed and the *if* omitted: *Were I you, I'd resign.*

subordinate clause In a sentence, a clause that is dependent on the main clause and cannot stand as a sentence on its own. A subordinate clause can relate to the main clause in an adjectival, an adverbial, or a noun way.

subpoena Spelling: remember the **oe**.

subsidence In both British and American English there are two pronunciations. One begins with a weak syllable like the beginning of *submit*, [sub-**sigh**-duhns]. The other has the stress on the first syllable, which is pronounced like the beginning of *submarine*, [**sub**-si-duhns]

substantial *or* **substantive** If a thing is **substantial** it is considerable or sizeable: *We need a substantial improvement in sales* (so that they are greater). If something is **substantive** it is real or actual: *We need a substantive improvement in sales* (not just a cosmetic improvement).

substitute *or* **replace** Either can be used when speaking of a matter of choice: *Substitute low-fat yoghurt for cream; Replace cream with low-fat yoghurt.* In the sense of putting something new in place of something old or broken, **replace** is normally used when the replacement is very similar to, or better than, the thing replaced: *We replaced the dead batteries* (with new ones of the same kind); *We replaced the typewriters with word processors.* **Substitute** implies that the replacement is not as good, or that it will be used only temporarily: *Finding the chain broken, he substituted an old piece of rope; It may be better to substitute plastic for china while the children are small.*

subtle Spelling: remember the **b.**

succeed Spelling: remember the double **c.**

success Spelling: remember the double **c.**

succinct Spelling: remember the double **c.**

suddenness Spelling: note the double **n.**

suede Spelling: remember the **ue.**

suffix A letter or group of letters added to the end of a word in order to show its tense or person: *-ed* in *passed; -es* in *goes;* to form the plural: *-ren* in *children;* to change the part of speech: *-ful* in *wonderful* (adjective); *wonderment* (noun); or form a new word: *-ist* in *sexist.* Common suffixes are *-ing;-ed;-ness;-less;-able.*

sullenness Spelling: note the double **n.**

sulphate US spelling: *sulfate.*

sulphide US spelling: *sulfide.*

sulphur US spelling: *sulfur.*

superintendent Spelling: note the ending **-ent.**

superlative The maximum degree of an adjective or adverb, created by the use of *most* or an *-est* ending: *largest; greatest; most surprising; most speedily; most unusually.*

supersede Spelling: note especially the ending **-sede**, not -*cede* like *precede*. The word derives from the Latin *supersedere*, meaning 'to sit above', and so is related to words such as *sedentary* and *sedan*.

supine See ⟩prone.

suppress Spelling: remember the double **p**.

surfeit Spelling: note the **ei**.

surliness Spelling: the **y** of *surly* changes to an **i**.

susceptible Spelling: note the **sc**.

swap *or* **swop** This word can be spelled either way.

swath (as in cutting hay). The main British pronunciation is [swoth], to rhyme with *moth*, although [sworth] is also heard. The alternative noun *swathe*, and the verb *swathe* (as in wrapping or bandaging) are both pronounced by British and American speakers to rhyme with *bathe*.

swop See ⟩swap.

syllable A unit of a word, when spoken, that contains a vowel sound or a vowel-like sound. *Photo* has two syllables; *photograph* has three syllables; *photography* has four syllables.

syllabus Spelling: remember the **y**.

symmetry Spelling: remember the **y** and the double **m**.

sympathy *or* **empathy** Sympathy (literally 'feeling with') is a compassion or commiseration with someone: *When he heard the news, he offered her his sympathy*; *She felt a great sense of sympathy for the homeless* (she pitied them). **Empathy** (literally 'feeling into') is the ability to understand another person's feelings and to put oneself in their position: *She felt a great sense of empathy for the homeless* (she knew what they were feeling and what it must be like).

syndrome Spelling: remember the **y**.

synonym Spelling: remember the two **y**s.

syrup Spelling: remember the **y**.

tableau Spelling: remember the ending **-eau**.

taboo *or* **tabu** This word can be spelled either way.

tacit Spelling: remember **c**, not **s**.

tailless Spelling: remember the double **l**.

taramasalata Spelling: remember no double letters.

tardiness Spelling: the **y** of *tardy* changes to an **i**.

targeted Spelling: note the single **t**, which is because the syllable is unstressed.

tariff Spelling: remember the single **r** and double **f**.

tarot Spelling: note the ending **-ot**.

tarragon Spelling: note the double **r**.

tassel Spelling: note the ending **-el**.

tastiness Spelling: the **y** of *tasty* changes to an **i**.

tattoo Spelling: note the double **t**.

tautology This is the name for a particular fault in expression, the unnecessary duplication of an idea using different words. In the phrase: *the former musical glories of an earlier time*, *former* is not needed; it means 'of an earlier time'. In the phrase: *the circumstances surrounding her death*, the word *circumstances* already means *conditions surrounding*, so it should be followed simply by *of*. Here are some further examples:

a new innovation; an amazing marvel; return the book back to the library; at this moment in time; the one single reason; the single most quoted reason; make a beeline straight there; an added bonus

It is noticeable that many tautological expressions are clichés. They come ready made along tired old grooves of expression. The reader may well wonder whether tired expression means tired ideas.

Some tautologies arise because the writer does not know the precise meaning of a word. An *innovation*, for example, is a 'new' idea or way of doing something, not just an idea or practice.

It is quite easy to introduce tautologies into a piece of writing when you are searching among various similar phrases for a way to express an idea, so it is wise to look out for them when you are checking a piece of writing.

temporary Spelling: remember the **ar**.

tenet Spelling: note the single **n**.

tense The form a verb takes to indicate action in the present, past, or future.

tepid Spelling: note the single **p**.

terrific Spelling: remember the double **r** and single **f**.

thankfully The use of *thankfully* to mean 'fortunately', 'let us be thankful (that)', is still disliked by many people, although it is becoming accepted. In this sense it is separated from the rest of the sentence by a comma. *Thankfully they went to their grandfather's that day* means that they went there full of gratitude; *Thankfully, they went to their grandfather's that day* means that it was fortunate that they did so; *They went to their grandfather's, thankfully, that day* means it was fortunate that they went on that particular day.

their *or* **they're** Their means 'of them', while **they're** is short for 'they are': *That's their house, over there, and they're in the garden right now*. See also ◊they/their/theirs.

thence See ◊hence.

they/their/theirs They is the third person plural pronoun, which means that it refers to more than one person. In the second half of the 20th century, however, it has become increasingly common to use it as an indefinite pronoun which could refer to just one person.

There is a range of indefinite words in English – *anybody, anyone; everybody, everyone; nobody, no one; somebody, someone; either, neither, each* – which traditionally have been used with the masculine singular pronoun: *If anyone finds my glasses, could he let me know?* In this role, the masculine pronoun notionally has an indefinite function, covering women as well as men.

However, it has come more and more to be seen as invidious to use a masculine pronoun to refer to women, and users of the language have been seeking an alternative. *He or she*, and *she or he*, are cumbersome, especially if they need to be repeated several times, and anyway they give precedence to males or females. Increasingly *they*, together with its possessive forms *their* and *theirs*, is becoming the preferred option: *If anyone finds my glasses, could they let me know?*

It is not yet completely established in standard English, and some people still object to it, but its usefulness is widely recognized, and it seems likely that in due course it will become generally accepted.

Remember that the third person plural possessive adjective is *their*: *They've sold their house*. Don't confuse it with the adverb *there*, 'in that place' or with *they're*, which is the shortened form of 'they are'.

The third person plural possessive pronoun is *theirs* (not their's): *If this is theirs, they'd better take it*.

they're See ◊their.

this *(Tuesday, etc)* Beware of possible ambiguity when using **this** with days of the week. *This Tuesday* will usually be taken to mean 'the Tuesday of this week', but if the time of speaking is midway between two Tuesdays, *this Tuesday* might refer to the one passed or the one to come. The same is true of **next** and **last**. If said on a Sunday, *next Tuesday* might be the day after tomorrow or the Tuesday of the following week; on a Thursday, *last Tuesday* could be the day before yesterday or the Tuesday of the previous week. Avoid using these terms in writing, as you do not know when it may be read; give the date.

threshold Spelling: note the single **h** in the middle.

thriftiness Spelling: the **y** of *thrifty* changes to an **i**.

tidiness Spelling: the **y** of *tidy* changes to an **i**.

timid *or* **timorous** Timid means shy or frightened: *'Do I go on now?' she asked, in a timid voice*; *He made a timid offer to help*. **Timorous** means much the same, but implies a reluctance or shrinking back: *The new tenants were too timorous to complain about the noise*; *The dog gave a few timorous barks on first facing the hedgehog*.

titillate Spelling: remember the single **t** and double **l**.

tobacco Spelling: remember the single **b** and double **c**.

toboggan Spelling: remember the single **b** and double **g**.

tomato Spelling: note that there is no **e** at the end.

torpor Spelling: note the ending **-or**.

torque Spelling: note the ending **-que**.

tortuous *or* **torturous** If something is **tortuous** it is full of twists and turns or long and complicated: *We climbed the tortuous path up the hill*; *The negotiations for the release of the hostages were protracted and tortuous*. If a thing is **torturous** it relates to torture: *Families of the trapped men waited in torturous silence for news*.

touchiness Spelling: the **y** of *touchy* changes to an **i**.

toward *or* **towards** Either form may be used in British English, although **towards** is more common. **Toward** is used in American English.

Tracey *or* **Tracy** This is usually a feminine name, but can also be a masculine name. Either spelling can be used for a girl or a boy.

trait The standard British pronunciation is [tray], the final **t** in the spelling being silent as in the original French word. However, [trayt], with the final **t** pronounced, is also an acceptable pronunciation. It is the only US pronunciation.

transcend Spelling: remember the **c**.

transferred Spelling: note the double **r**, unlike *transfer*.

transhipment Spelling: note there is only one **s**.

transitive verb a verb that can take a direct object: *Alison loved her cat*. The action passes directly from the subject to the object noun or pronoun. A verb that cannot take a direct object is an intransitive verb.

transparent The most common British pronunciation has the stress on the middle syllable, which is pronounced like the beginning of *sparrow*. Some people pronounce the first syllable [trarn] and some pronounce the second syllable [pear]. The US pronunciation starts with [trarn] and ends with [errant].

trauma Two pronunciations are standard in Britain, [**tror**-mer], the most usual, and standard in medical English, and [**trow**-mer].

tremor Spelling: note the ending **-or**.

trestle Spelling: remember the **t**.

tricycle Spelling: remember **i** then **y**.

troop *or* **troupe** Remember that **troop** means a group of people or animals. Use **troupe** if you mean a company of actors or performers. See also ◊trooper.

trooper *or* **trouper** Use **trooper** if you mean a soldier. Use **trouper** if you mean a loyal or dependable person. See also ◊troop.

troupe See ◊troop.

trouper See ◊trooper.

truculent This is pronounced [**truck**-yer-luhnt] and rhymes with *succulent*.

truism Spelling: note there is no **e** after the **u**.

truly Spelling: note there is no **e** after the **u**.

trustworthiness Spelling: the **y** of *trustworthy* changes to an **i**.

tryst Spelling: note the **y**.

tsar See ◊czar.

tubbiness Spelling: the **y** of *tubby* changes to an **i**.

twelfth Spelling: remember the **f**.

type See ◊kind.

tyranny Spelling: remember the **y**.

tyre US spelling: *tire*.

tzar See ◊czar.

U

ugliness Spelling: the **y** of *ugly* changes to an **i**.

ukulele Spelling: remember the two **us** and two **es**.

umbilical The standard pronunciation is [um-**bill**-ickle] with the stress on the second syllable. [Umbill-**lie**-kle] is also used, if the word is not before a noun.

underrated Spelling: note the double **r**.

unduly Spelling: note that there is no **e** after the second **u**.

uneasiness Spelling: the **y** of *uneasy* changes to an **i**.

unevenness Spelling: remember the double **n**.

unfriendliness Spelling: the **y** of *unfriendly* changes to an **i**.

uninterested See ◊disinterested.

unique Unique means 'being the only one of its kind, without equal or like'. It is sometimes used with adverbs like *very, more, rather, somewhat*, or *comparatively*, which dilute its meaning to 'unusual' or 'exceptional'. Many people object to this, and it is best to avoid it, especially in formal writing.

United Kingdom See ◊Britain.

unlike This can precede a noun or a pronoun: *She is quite unlike her brother; A book unlike any other*. It can also introduce a whole clause: *Unlike those in poorer countries, people here seldom go hungry*. Do not say *Unlike in poorer countries, people here seldom go hungry*, as *people* is not being compared to anything.

   Make sure that the things said to be unlike each other can actually be compared: a sentence such as *Unlike Colin, Jacky's talent is for business* compares *Colin* with *Jacky's talent*, not with Jacky herself. Use *Unlike Colin's, Jacky's talent is for business* or, more elegantly, *Unlike Colin, Jacky has a talent for business*.

unnamed Spelling: note the double **n**.

unnatural Spelling: note the double **n**.

unnecessary Spelling: note the double **n**, single **c** and double **s**.

unnerving Spelling: note the double **n**.

unsightliness Spelling: the **y** of *unsightly* changes to an **i**.

unskilful Spelling: note the single **ls**. US spelling: *unskilful*.

unsociable *or* **unsocial** Unsociable is used of someone who does not wish to be friendly or to talk to others: *He's very unsociable, and doesn't like parties*. Unsocial can also mean this, but more commonly refers to something that is in some sense anti-social: *Anne's new job involves unsocial hours, so that she has to work in the evenings or at weekends*.

until Spelling: remember only one **l** (unlike *till*).

unusual Spelling: note that there is no **h** after the **s**.

unwanted *or* **unwonted** Someone or something **unwanted** is not wanted: *What do you do with your unwanted presents?* Something **unwonted** is out of the ordinary or unusual: *That was an unwonted liberty on your part*.

upper case See ◊case, upper and lower.

Uranus In British English the traditional pronunciation [yer-**eh**-nus] is giving way to a pronunciation with the stress on the first syllable [**yure**-ernus]. The US pronunciation is [yure-**eh**-nus].

used to *Used to* expresses the idea of something we did in the past but no longer do: *When I was a child, we used to go to Scarborough for our holidays*.

Using *used to* in questions and negative sentences can present problems. The usual way of turning a sentence like *He used to snore* into a question is with the word *did*. This is straightforward in spoken English, but there are two possible ways of writing it. The more logical is: *Did he use to snore?* The alternative, *Did he used to snore?*, is becoming more accepted, but it still strikes many people as odd. You can also make a question by reversing the word order: *Used he to snore?* But this is becoming less common.

The usual way of making *used to* negative is with *didn't*. But again, there's a problem with how to write it. *He didn't use to snore* is more widely acceptable than *He didn't used to snore*. You can also put *not* after *used*, although this is becoming less common: *He used not to snore*. The contracted written form is *usedn't*, not *usen't*. You can avoid any difficulty by using *never*: *He never used to snore*.

For negative questions, you can say: *Didn't he use* (or used) *to snore?* or *Usedn't he to snore?* (the uncontracted form of this, *Used he not to snore?*, is rather pompous and old-fashioned).

utilize Avoid using *utilize* to mean simply 'use'. *Utilize* is best confined to the sense 'put something to an unusual or unexpected practical use': *The children made a tent, utilizing the clothes-line and some old curtains*. Even in this sense, it is nearly always possible, and more elegant, to say *use*.

vaccinate Spelling: remember the double **c**.

vacillate Spelling: remember the single **c** and double **l**.

vacuum Spelling: remember the double **u**.

vague Spelling: note the ending **-gue**.

valet Spelling: note the ending **-et**.

vanilla Spelling: note the single **n** and double **l**.

vaporous Spelling: note that there is no **u** before the **r**.

variegated Spelling: remember **e** in the middle, not **a**.

vegetable Spelling: remember the second **e**.

venal See ◊venial.

vendor US spelling: *vender*.

venial *or* **venal** A **venial** offence is a slight or excusable one: *Some dogs are punished for relatively venial offences*. A **venal** offence is a serious one that involves corruption and bribery: *The candidate committed the venal offence of bribing colleagues to vote for him*.

venue Spelling: remember the ending **-ue**.

veranda *or* **verandah** This word can be spelled either way.

verb This is a grammatical part of speech for what someone does: *I work*, experiences: *I feel silly*, or is: *I am old*. Verbs involve the grammatical categories of number, mood, and tense. Many verbs are formed with affixes: *prison, imprison; light, enlighten; pure, purify*. Some words function as both nouns and verbs: *crack; run*, as both adjectives and verbs: *clean*, and as nouns, adjectives, and verbs: *foul*.

vermilion Spelling: note there is only one **l**.

veterinary Spelling: note the **er** which is often not pronounced.

vice (meaning a tool). US spelling: *vise*.

vicious Spelling: note **ci**, not **sh**.

victuals Spelling: remember the **c**.

vigorous Spelling: note that there is no **u** before the **r**.

vilify The stress is on the first syllable, which is pronounced like the beginning of *village*. Spelling: note the single **l**.

villain *or* **villein** Spelling: remember that a **villain** is a bad person, and a **villein** is a serf in a feudal country.

vineyard Spelling: remember the **e**, as in *vine*.

violoncello Spelling: note that it is not *violin-* .

virulent Spelling: note the single **r**.

viscount Spelling: remember the **s**.

visor *or* **vizor** This word can be spelled either way.

Vivian Strictly speaking this is a masculine name, with an alternative spelling *Vyvyan*. The feminine forms are *Vivien*, *Vivienne*, or *Vivianne*. However, while the feminine forms are not used for men, all the forms are now used for women.

vizor See ◊visor.

vol-au-vent This word comes from the French and literally means 'flight in the wind'.

vouch See ◊avow.

vowel Any of the five letters of the English alphabet *a; e; i; o; u.*

waive Note the spelling of this word: *I waived my rights to the house.* Do not confuse it with *wave* (as in, for example, *I waved my hand* or *the waves of the sea*).

wake, waken See ▷awake, awaken.

walnut Spelling: note the single **l**.

wanness The stress is on the first syllable, which is pronounced to rhyme with *Ron*[**won**-nuhs]. Spelling: note the double **n**.

wantonness Spelling: note the double **n**.

wariness Spelling: the **y** of *wary* changes to an **i**.

was *or* **were** In the ordinary past tense of the verb *to be*, **was** is the first and third person singular: *I was late*, and **were** is the second person singular and the plural: *You were right*. It is not acceptable in standard English to use *were* for the first and third person singular: *I were late*, and *was* for the second person singular and the plural: *You was right*.

In the past subjunctive, however, the situation is more fluid. Historically the past subjunctive of *be* is **were** for all persons, singular and plural: *I wish she were here*; *Suppose I were rich*; *If only they weren't so expensive*. It is quite common, though, to use *was* instead of *were* for the first and third person singular: *I wish she was here*; *Suppose I was rich*. This is perfectly acceptable in colloquial English, but in formal writing it is better to stick to *were*. Remember that the fixed phrase *as it were* cannot be changed – never *as it was*. See also ▷subjunctive.

wave See ▷waive.

weariness Spelling: the **y** of *weary* changes to an **i**.

wearisome Spelling: the **y** of *weary* changes to an **i**.

Wednesday Spelling: remember the **d**.

weightiness Spelling: the **y** of *weighty* changes to an **i**.

weir Spelling: note the **ei**.

weird Spelling: note the **ei**.

whence See ◊hence.

whetstone Spelling: note the **h**.

which *or* **that** *Which* and *that* are both relative pronouns: they introduce ◊relative clauses. The main difference between them is that while **which** can introduce both restrictive relative clauses: *The zebra which the lion picked on was clearly sick* and non-restrictive relative clauses: *The zebra, which lives in southern Africa, is related to the horse*, **that** can introduce only restrictive relative clauses: *The zebra that the lion picked on was clearly sick.*

Which and *that* are equally acceptable in restrictive relative clauses; *that* is perhaps the less formal of the two.

Which can be used after a preposition: *Is this the coat for which you paid £300?*, but *that* cannot (you cannot say *Is this the coat for that you paid £300?* – although you can say *Is this the coat that you paid £300 for?*).

Which can refer to both nouns and pronouns: *This is the one which I prefer* and whole sentences: *He's off sick, which is rather a shame*, but *that* can refer only to nouns and pronouns: *This is the one that I prefer.*

When two separate relative clauses in the same sentence refer to the same noun, they should both be introduced by either *which* or *that* (or by *who*, if the noun refers to a person). *Which* is perhaps preferable to *that* in these parallel clauses: *This is the system which Parsloe invented, and which has been used in the service for over twenty years.* Don't mix *which* clauses with *that* clauses: *This is the system that Parsloe invented, and which has been used in the service for over twenty years* is not to be recommended.

Take care not to begin a relative clause with *and which* when there was no previous *which* clause for the *and* to relate to: *This is the system invented by Parsloe, and which has been used in the service for over twenty years* is not grammatical.

while *and* **whilst** These are more or less interchangeable in British English, although some people feel that *whilst* is more formal. **Whilst** is slightly more common when the meaning is 'whereas' or 'although': *Whilst she is new to the job, she learns quickly*, but: *While she is new, perhaps you would help her.* In American English, *whilst* is not used.

whir *or* **whirr** This word can be spelled either way but in American English *whir* is preferred.

whisky *or* **whiskey** *Whisky* is the spelling for Scotch whisky, while *whiskey* is the spelling for Irish, and also the US spelling.

whither This word (meaning 'where to') is easy to misspell. Remember the **h**, as in *where*, and do not confuse it with *wither* which means 'to dry up'.

whizz *or* **whiz** This word can be spelled either way.

who *or* **whom** Who is the subject of a verb: *Who said that?* **Whom** is the object of a verb or preposition: *To whom can we turn?*

So far so good. But *whom* is quite a formal word, and many people feel uncomfortable using it in ordinary contexts.

There are some circumstances in which you can avoid it. In questions, it is acceptable to use *who* instead: *Who have you told?* And in questions ending with a preposition, it is preferable to use *who*: *Who were you talking to?* (It would sound very stilted to ask *Whom were you talking to?* or *To whom were you talking?*).

It is sometimes possible to use *that* instead of *whom*: *He is a man that you can trust.*

And in non-formal contexts you can simply leave out the *whom*: *He is a man you can trust.*

People who are aware of the 'correctness' of *whom* can be tempted to use it in circumstances where it does not belong. This is particularly common where there is a short parenthetic clause: *A man who I had supposed was dead* is correct, *A man whom I had supposed was dead* is not. If you take out the parenthetic clause (here, *I had supposed*), you can see that *who* is the subject of the verb *was*, so it cannot be *whom*.

There is also a tendency to use *whom* as the complement of the verb *to be*. This should be resisted: *Do you realize who I am?* is right, *Do you realize whom I am?* is wrong.

who's See ◊whose.

wholly This word (meaning 'completely') is easy to misspell. Do not confuse it with *holy* (meaning 'sacred').

whooping (as in *whooping cough*). Spelling: remember the **w**.

whose *or* **who's** Whose means 'of whom': *Whose house is that? I don't know whose it is.* **Who's** is a shortened form of 'who has' or *who is*: *Who's got my pen? Let's see who's winning.*

wildebeest Spelling: note **ee**, not **ea**.

wilful Spelling: note the single **ls**. US spelling: *willful*.

wiliness Spelling: the **y** of *wily* changes to an **i**.

wiriness Spelling: the **y** of *wiry* changes to an **i**.

-wise This suffix originally meant 'in this manner or way', and formed words such as *slantwise; crosswise; otherwise*. In recent years it has often been used to mean 'in this respect', 'as regards': *Moneywise, the job's much better, although it's not as interesting*. This is useful and acceptable in informal speech, although some people dislike it. Writingwise, avoid it.

wistaria *or* **wisteria** This word can be spelled either way.

wither See ▷whither.

withhold Spelling: note the two **hs**.

woke, woken See ▷awake, awaken.

woman See ▷girl, lady.

wondrous Spelling: note that there is no **e** after the **d**.

woodenness Spelling: note the double **n**.

woollen Spelling: note the double **l**. US spelling: *woolen*.

woolliness Spelling: note the double **l**, and the **i**.

wrack See ▷rack.

wraith Spelling: remember the **w**.

wrath The standard current British pronunciation is [roth], but some older well educated people say [rawth]. The US pronunciation is [rath], to rhyme with *Kath*.

wreak Spelling: remember the **w**.

wretch This word (meaning a pitiable person) is easy to misspell. Do not confuse it with *retch* (meaning to strain as if to vomit).

xenophobia Spelling: remember that it begins with **x**, not **z**.

xerox Spelling: remember that it begins with **x**, not **z**.

Xmas This abbreviation has a very limited range of acceptable use. There is really no reason to use it in speech, as it is no shorter than *Christmas*, and it should not be used in formal writing. Many Christians dislike it, although the **X** is not just an arbitrary letter but represents *chi* (χ), the initial letter of Christ's name in Greek. It is probably best to think of **Xmas** as an abbreviation like *Thurs* or *Fri*, and avoid using it anywhere you would write *Thursday* or *Friday* in full.

xylophone Spelling: remember that it begins with **x**, not **z**.

yacht Spelling: note the **ach**.

yearn Spelling: remember the **ea**.

yeoman Spelling: remember the **eo**.

yoghurt, yoghourt *or* **yogurt** This word can be spelled in all three ways. The standard British pronunciation has a first syllable that rhymes with *jog*. The second syllable is weak, like the end of *nugget*. The US pronunciation start with [yo] as in *yo-yo*.

yolk This word (meaning the yellow part of an egg) is easy to misspell. Do not confuse it with *yoke*, which is what joins a pair of oxen together, or part of a dress.

your *or* **you're** **Your** means 'belonging to you': *Is this your pen? I won't forget your birthday.* **You're** means 'you are': *Look out, you're spilling your tea.*

yours *Yours* is a pronoun. It means 'the one(s) belonging to you': *Is this car yours?* Remember, it's *yours*, not *your's*.

zaniness Spelling: the **y** of *zany* changes to an **i**.

zealous Spelling: remember the **ea**, as in *jealous*.

zephyr Spelling: note the **ph** and the **y**.

zoology Both [zoe-**oll**-ogy] and [zoo-**oll**-ogy] are standard pronunciations. Purists prefer the first, the beginning of which rhymes with *toe*.

zucchini The US word for *courgette*. Spelling: note the **cch**.